TABLE OF CONTENTS

ABOUT US

Veterans Radio is dedicated to all the men and women who have served or are currently serving in the Armed Forces of the United States of America. Our mission is to see that the world appreciates what extraordinary things ordinary people have done to gain and preserve the freedom we assume everyone enjoys—and the ultimate price that is often paid.

Veterans Radio tells veterans stories and experiences, not only while in the service, but afterwards as well. Interviews with guest speakers and authors are a weekly feature. The content of the programs on **Veterans Radio** is ultimately determined by our listeners.

Veterans Radio feels it is time for our communities to know who among their neighbors was willing to pay the ultimate price to preserve and protect their basic freedoms. **Veterans Radio** will act as an advocate for veteran's issues. Politics has no place in determining what is fair for America's veterans. **Veterans Radio** just wants our politicians to keep their promises. We encourage our listeners to get involved in the political process and to make our voices heard.

Dale Throneberry—Dale is the unofficial commander of the **Veterans Radio** crew. He is originally from New Jersey where he grew up on the Jersey Shore. His military experience includes basic training at Ft. Polk, Louisiana, Army Aviation Training at Ft. Wolters, Texas and Ft. Rucker, Alabama. He completed his tour in Vietnam as a CW2 pilot with the 195th Assault Helicopter Company from December 1968 to December 1969. After completing his tour, he returned to The Army Aviation School at Fort Rucker, Alabama and completed his enlistment as an instructor pilot until his discharge in May of 1971.

Thanks to the GI Bill, Dale was able to complete his BA in Education and MA in Communication at The University of Michigan. He has worked in education and the insurance business since graduating in 1975.

Veterans Radio was a dream Dale had years ago and he's very grateful to have the opportunity to make the dream come true.

Dale currently lives in Ann Arbor, MI with his wife Jane and feels fortunate to have his son and family, including a grandson, live nearby. You can reach him at dale@veteransradio.net

Bob Gould—Bob Gould was born and grew up in Northwest Detroit. He joined the army the July after graduating from Redford High School.

Bob completed his basic training at Fort Knox, Kentucky and was then sent to Fort Riley, Kansas for Advanced Infantry Training. Bob became proficient as a Forward Observer for an 81 MM mortar platoon.

In July, 1962, Bob completed Basic Airborne Training and was assigned to the 101st Airborne Division. There he completed his two-year enlistment as a medic in the 326 Medical Battalion.

After service, Bob went on to have two sons and graduated with a Masters in Education degree from The University of Michigan. Currently, Bob lives in Ann Arbor, Michigan and is President of Small Business Benefits, plays recreational hockey, and loves old fashioned rock and roll. You can reach him at bob@veteransradio.net.

Jim Fausone, Attorney at Law—After Jim Fausone served his country, he went to law school on the G.I. Bill. He married his college sweetheart, Carol Ann, who was a lieutenant in the USAF at the time and retired a Brigadier General.

Jim is a graduate of the University of Michigan College of Engineering and an honors graduate of the Gonzaga University School of Law.

Jim is admitted before the U.S. Court of Appeals for Veterans Claims, United States Supreme Court, Michigan Supreme Court, as well as various Federal District Courts. He is a member of the National Organization for Veteran Advocates (NOVA). He serves on numerous civic boards.

He has built Legal Help for Veterans, PLLC into one of the premier veteran disability firms in the country. He has worked closely with veteran service organizations and veteran-centric organizations. Jim is a frequent writer, blogger, and lecturer on veteran topics. He organizes the largest Veterans Benefits Summit in Michigan each fall with hundreds of veterans in attendance. You can reach him at jim@legalhelpforveterans.com.

Brigadier General (ret.) Carol Ann Fausone—General Fausone served her country for 34 years from 1977–2011. From 2003-2011 she served as the Assistant Adjutant General of Veterans Affairs, Department of Military and Veterans Affairs, State of Michigan.

From 2001-2005, General Fausone served as the Assistant for Mobilization and Reserve Affairs working directly with the Deputy Assistant Secretary of Defense for Health Affairs, Force Health Protection and Readiness. Serving in this capacity, she assisted in developing and implementing programs, policy, and operations for Reserve Affairs.

General Fausone graduated from the University of Michigan School of Nursing in 1975. In 1983 and 1995, she completed a Master of Science in Administration and a Master of Science in Nursing from Madonna University in Livonia, Michigan.

Carol Ann continues serving by "Taking Care of Our American Heroes and their Families" to obtain the benefits they deserve. She owns The Veteran Advocate, LLC and works with Legal Help for Veterans, PLLC. She can be reached at general@legalhelpforveterans.com.

 **Gary Lillie** was a huge supporter of Veterans Radio who became an on-air personality. Gary cared deeply about veterans issues and Veterans Radio was a natural outlet.

Gary Lillie was born in Detroit, Michigan and completed his high school education in Detroit.

Gary enlisted in the Navy and became a Seabee after basic and volunteered for Vietnam. A Seabee is a member of the US Navy Construction Battalion (CB).

Gary was involved in setting up numerous camp sites for the Marines while he was in Vietnam. Although his Unit experienced many overhead attacks, his Unit did not experience any casualties.

When he returned to Michigan, he had lots of problems that led to heavy drinking. It was not until 1989 that he sobered up. Gary worked as a carpenter when he first returned home but eventually ended up in commercial real estate. Gary died at the age of 70 while taking a late night walk, when struck by a drunk driver.

Gary had made peace with his Vietnam service and a peacetime trip back there brought him perspective. He was a dedicated friend, producer and host for Veterans Radio. He is missed.

VETERANS RADIO

You can find us at www.veteransradio.net. The stories that are told here are from the over 500 stories in the Veterans Radio archive that can be found on our website.

You can follow Veterans Radio and its weekly programs by "liking" Veterans Radio on Facebook.

You can listen live to the weekly show on the internet from your computer, laptop, smartphone or tablet.

THE PROCESS

This book features edited portions of programs aired by Veterans Radio over the years. The entire audio program can be heard in the archives section of www.veteransradio.net.

As part of the editorial process, the transcripts have been created, some grammar adjusted, and sentence structure rewritten. Any misstatements or misspellings are the fault of the editors.

The editors have also added information about the program topic from Wikipedia and hereby acknowledge the copyright of that source for this information. The block quotes at the start of each chapter are from various Wikipedia pages, which is an open source encyclopedia, on the internet.

CHAPTER 1
SPOOKS AND SPIES

Bob Gould interviewed author James Wolterman about "Spooks and Spies" in July 2013.

"The **United States Army Security Agency** (ASA) was the United States Army's signal intelligence branch. The Latin motto of the Army Security Agency was *Semper Vigilis* (Vigilant Always), which echoes Thomas Jefferson's declaration that "The price of freedom is eternal vigilance." The Agency existed between 1945 and 1976 and was the successor to Army signal intelligence operations dating back to World War I. ASA was under the operational control of the Director of the National Security Agency (DIRNSA), located at Fort Meade, Maryland; but had its own tactical commander at Headquarters, ASA, Arlington Hall Station, VA. Besides intelligence gathering, it had responsibility for the security of Army communications and for electronic countermeasures operations. In 1977, the ASA was merged with the US Army's Military Intelligence component to create the United States Army Intelligence and Security Command (INSCOM)."

Vietnam War

"Although not officially serving under the ASA name, covertly designated as Radio Research, ASA personnel of the 3rd Radio Research Unit were among the earliest U.S. military personnel in Vietnam; 3rd later grew to become the 509th Radio Research Group.

ASA personnel processing out of sensitive operations were debriefed and signed a document specifying a forty-year elapsed time before they could discuss what they had done or observed." Four decades have past and the stories can now be told.

July 2013

Gould: Tell us about your service in Vietnam.

James Wolterman: I was a Morse code interceptor, but let me back up just a second. If you and I had this conversation last year, I couldn't tell you anything because when I got out in 1972, when I was debriefed, I actually signed a document stating that I could not talk about what I did for 40 years. More guys who have served in the United States Army Security Agency (ASA) around the world are coming out with books. Almost monthly new memoirs and new books are coming out with what the ASA did in Vietnam and around the world. If people are interested to find out, just search ASA on the internet.

Gould: Is the ASA directly going to the Joint Chiefs of Staff, what is the chain of command for orders for the ASA?

Wolterman: The ASA was taken down in 1976 and became part of the National Security Agency. The ASA was formed in 1945 under the command of the National Security Agency but they actually had a tactical military commander in Arlington, VA. The initial mission of the ASA during the Cold War time was to gather intelligence on the Russians, Chinese and their allies around the world. The ASA formed major military listening posts all over the world. In 1965, the Army said these guys are doing a great job, we would like them under our command. Then the ASA became under the US Army command but were reporting to the National Security Agency. Every post around the world there was a National Security Agency technical advisor. So it was really working together with the civilians and the Army to get the communications needed, getting back to the proper channels to the people who made the decisions.

Gould: The first battlefield fatality of the Vietnam War was Specialist Fourth Class James Davis who was killed in December 1961 and he was assigned to the third radio Research Unit at Tan Son Nhut Air Base near Saigon and there were 92 other members of his unit. You guys were targets right?

Wolterman: Without a doubt. What's the first thing you want to do, you want to get rid of the people who are spying on you, who know what you are going to do before you know what you are going to do.

If you don't have intelligence, how can you perform? The ASA in Vietnam was one of the greatest intelligence gathering units in the history of the US. We took this very seriously. We understood the consequences if we talked. There were so many advances that we knew were coming out later on as far as intelligence gathering.

Gould: Like what?

Wolterman: We could actually pinpoint where you stood if you had a radio transmitter within 3 square meters of you anywhere in the world.

Gould: Would you send those to coordinators who would send out a strike?

Wolterman: That was definitely one of the parts. The thing you have to understand in intelligence is you want to monitor your enemy and if everything is normal, that's acceptable. What you are looking for is the abnormal. Is someone moving? Why is he moving and where is he moving to? What we do is monitor communications. As we are monitoring their communications, we keep track of exactly where they are. So, if the next day, we hear nothing, we want to know why. And it might be 2 or 3 days and then they pop up again. It shows they moved 40 miles. Why did they move 40 miles? We actually have analysts who did it, but it goes up the chain of command. This is where this unit was on this date and here they are today. Is it a supply unit, a combat unit? That's the kind of things we did 24 hours today, 7 days a week, 365 days a year.

Gould: How long was your shift?

Wolterman: 12 hours a day. When I last left there, I think we had one day off every 65-70 days.

Gould: You ate at the desk?

Wolterman: Yes, you did.

Gould: What was the room like that you were in?

Wolterman: The room was positioned with guys sitting at a desk with a receiver with headsets on and a mill in front of them. A mill being a typewriter with all capital letters on it. There would be 8-10 people and you would have a room supervisor in case somebody had trouble. They had a mission. They had people that they had to track every day to find out where they were at and if they didn't find that person, they knew how to search and find them. They were so good that they could tell their man by his transmitter. Not his call sign, his transmitter.

Wolterman: You are not transmitting, you are listening to their transmitter through your headset. They are sending call signs to identify themselves and identify who they want to talk to. So if you can't find him, he might change his call sign just to mess you up. These guys were good enough that they could pick up their transmitter and say that's him, I know that's him. The people behind him believe him enough they would come in and follow any kind of communications that were written and as soon as they were done, they would tear it off and bring it to the analyst.

Gould: Were there any windows in the room?

Wolterman: No.

Gould: Was it a block or was it a tent when you were out in Vietnam? Were you always in a permanent building?

Wolterman: There was everything. There were main stations. One main station in the north part of Vietnam and one in the south. Then we had guys in what we called DSU Units (Direct Support Units). They might be in a little camper and there would be 2 guys in there out in the middle of the field living in bunkers with the MP surrounding them and guarding them. There were guys up in helicopters flying around, trying to locate people directly. There were guys in airplanes listening and following. If the enemy popped up, we had a helicopter and airplane there in a matter of minutes to find out where they are at, what they are doing because they didn't want to be found. When we heard that transmitter, we would relay that to the helicopters and airplanes and they would get there as soon as possible.

Gould: One of the things that led to so many successes in World War II were the breaking of the codes of the Germans and Japanese.

We knew about the attack that was coming to an area near midway. You told me that you folks broke a code. Tell me about that.

Wolterman: The enemy knew that we were monitoring them. It isn't easy to change your code. It has to be something that is structured and most of your codes are based on an algorithm, something to do with math. I'm sitting there and all these call signs are wrong and all the traffic coming across is not normal so we know they changed their code. At that point, everybody is heightened. This is handed from high command, everyone down to the guy right outside your gate when the rockets are out that night or throw a mortar at you. They all change so we have to find out how they changed their code and I want to talk about the personnel who did that. These are people with Master's Degrees, with Doctorate Degrees. The ASA had the best of the best and they would take the information that we were pulling in off of the air and they would be waiting for us to transmit and they would run back and in 24 hours they broke the new code.

Gould: So there was a common code, was it the North Vietnamese, whose code was it?

Wolterman: It's all done on Morse code. They are sent on Da dah Alpha. You've heard SOS? That's how it's all sent across the air. It's sent in five letter groups and within those five letter groups is a message or a word and you have to break out what it is. So once you have the code, you can read what we call clear text like its plain as day. If you don't have the code, it's just a bunch of letters.

Gould: Your responsibility in this facility is to interpret these codes, is that correct?

Wolterman: Yes, we actually intercepted the messages and then the room behind us would be the cryptanalyst and they would take the code and break it down and read it. That's where you had your NSA technical advisor and they would make the decisions.

Gould: Were you a "ditty bopper?"

Wolterman: Yes and proud to say it. What a ditty bopper was is we were the person sitting at that position copying the communications that they enemy was sending to each other.

Gould: Was a "hog" something that was the same?

Wolterman: Yes, same thing. The hogs were earlier before I came overseas. They called them hogs and then for some reason, we called them ditty boppers.

Gould: We are talking about intercepting these Morse codes.

Wolterman: Lack of intelligence. The same thing, we didn't believe the Japanese were going to bomb Pearl Harbor. We ignored it. The intelligence is there. It's how you interpret it and what you believe. We provided the intelligence to the people above. Did they believe that? Apparently not. But the intelligence was there. A unit like that does not move without communications. The communications were intercepted, were picked up, they were triangulated, they were place where they were at. If someone above does not believe it, I'm sorry.

Gould: The first rocket attack at Phu Bai. Tell us about that.

Wolterman: I was 18 when I got to Vietnam. We were flying into Thompson Air Force Base, and as we were coming down, it was night, and the plane jerked right back up in the air. The pilot comes over and says we are taking ground flak. What we are going to do is make a hot landing and you will see flashlights at bunkers, and you will go down the slides and you run to those bunkers as fast as you can once we are on the ground. Would you be scared? I couldn't even talk. Two months later, I'm up north in Phu Bai and I'm sleeping in my tent on my cot and all of the sudden the siren goes off. I didn't know exactly because I wasn't there long, what I was supposed to do. The rocket hit right over the blast wall from where our tent was and the shrapnel was going through the top of my tent. I rolled out on the floor and am crawling on the ground. All I have is my skivvies on, nothing else because it's 100 and something degrees over there. I crawled into a drainage ditch. I think I'm in the trench line and this NCO comes over to me and says "Boy, what the heck are you doing?" I said "I'm in the trench line" and was ranting and raving. He told me to "get back there and get your hard hat on, your flap jacket and rifle and get over in that trench line." I never slept that night, needless to say.

Gould: When you were out in the field, did you have protection? While these guys were protecting you, were you still attacked when you were out in the field?

Wolterman: In the field, it would be more mortar attacks than rocket attacks. Although rocket attacks were further away. Everybody out in the field was attacked at one time or another. The ASA actually had their own MPs who would protect us. We were also attached to bigger military units like we were attached to the 101st Airborne, we were attached to Fifth Mechanized Unit, so we would work with them and they would help protect us on our outer perimeters. It was a joint venture. We were feeding them the intelligence, they were protecting us.

Gould: Were you in a personnel carrier?

Wolterman: I was not. You're actually in a little house trailer. It's a truck that is set up with all the communications equipment inside of it. And you pull it, and sandbag around it, and you build bunkers around it and that's where you're at for a while. Or you can live on top of a hill inside a bunker. You needed to get close the enemy to get their communications. Guys risk their lives every day out in those units. Those were heroes. These are the guys that served in silence. We never heard of ASA before. These are the guys that went out there and did that every single day. Out there it was 24 hour shifts because when you were at your position, you were catnapping and watching for the enemy to come.

Gould: There is a way, and I don't know the term, that they could pick up your signal and trace it back to where you were. Were they able to find out and pinpoint where you were?

Wolterman: They never had the equipment that we had. They would pick up radio transmissions and get it to a point, but they weren't as good as we were. Could they do it that way? Yes, but it's hard to hide what we had. So when you have to clean an area to pull a truck and build a bunker, they know you're there. They had their own spies. They didn't have to have that much intelligence to see us.

Gould: I hesitated in using the word "spy." What do you feel about that?

Wolterman: Everyone thinks that if you talk spy, you talk cloak and dagger. This wasn't cloak and dagger. We were Morse code interceptors. We spied on their communications. We took their interceptions and we used it against them.

Gould: Tell us about that organization – Old Spooks and Spies.
Wolterman: It's a military organization of most of the guys who had spent time in Vietnam and like to sit back and talk about it.

Everyone asks, why do you like to hash over the past? I tell people that we were never so alive in our lives. Our adrenalin was pumping all the time while we were over there. We bonded like people don't understand how you bond. It's fun and it's a release. When we came back home, there were not flag-waving people when we came home. It was the opposite. When I came to San Francisco the first time, there were people yelling and protesting against us. So that made us a tighter group. We did this because we served our country and we are proud that we served our country and that is what makes us closer and that is what makes that organization so good.

Gould: Mortar attack in Quong Tri, why don't you let us know about that.

Wolterman: I was up in Quong Tri, that was another support unit that we had from our main base. It was like 2 o'clock in the morning and they didn't have urinals, we all know they had a bomb casing in the ground, and that's what you did do relieve yourself. So, I'm standing doing that and in comes a mortar. I hear it come in and it lands about 30 feet away from me. I am standing there waiting to die, the most peaceful feeling I have ever had in my life. I was ready to go and all of the sudden, something said to me it's not your time. At that instance, another mortar hit about 40 yards away from me and the guy came out, grabbed me and threw me on the ground. The mortar did not go off, the first one that landed next to me. The EOD Team came over (that's the demolition team) within hours and closed off the area. The captain calls me the next morning and says

"You're a lucky boy." I said "I know that." And he said "No, you don't understand, that firing pin ignited, it didn't go off, it should have gone off."

That's been a defining moment for me my whole life.

CHAPTER 2
VIETNAM POWS

In all wars, Killed In Action (KIA) deserve our preservation of their memories. The Missing in Action (MIA) require our constant vigilance to recover and return them to their families. The Prisoners of War (POW) require us to tell their stores.

Dale Throneberry interviewed Vietnam POW Robert C. Jones in June 2013. Mr. Jones has given interviews to the Veterans History Project and the POW Network. The former is extensive and can be found online.

"Following the Paris Peace Accords of 1973, 591 American Prisoners of War (POWs) were returned during Operation Homecoming.

The U.S. listed about 1,350 Americans as prisoners of war or missing in action and roughly 1,200 Americans reported killed in action and body not recovered. Many of these were airmen who were shot down over North Vietnam or Laos. Investigations of these incidents have involved determining whether the men involved survived their shoot down; if they did not survive, then they considered efforts to recover their remains. POW/MIA activists played a role in pushing the U.S. government to improve its efforts in resolving the fates of the missing. Progress in doing so was slow until the mid-1980s, when relations between the U.S. and Vietnam began to improve and more cooperative efforts were undertaken.

Normalization of U.S. relations with Vietnam in the mid-1990s was a culmination of this process."

June 2013

Throneberry: You go off to West Point from Chatham High School, and after your 4 years there, you did something unusual.

Jones: In those days, you could take a commission in another branch besides the Army. In those days, maybe 10% were allowed to choose another branch and so I had always wanted to be a pilot. My dad was a pilot in WWII. I was lucky enough to be able to choose the Air Force so at graduation, I received a commission as a Second Lieutenant. From there went to pilot training. It's 1965, right in the middle of Vietnam, they needed pilots and a number of us went to pilot training. After one year of pilot training, I was fortunate enough to be assigned to fly the F4 Phantom which is a Mach 2 fighter.

Throneberry: This is twice the speed of sound?

Jones: Twice the speed of sound and had a top speed of 1600 mph. It was an all-around fighter. It could bomb, it could do air-to-air, it could do about anything. After pilot training, I had to go to another Air Force base, Eglin Air Force Base in Florida, to learn how to fly the F4 and to learn how to deliver the ordinance and everything else.

Throneberry: How did you end up in Thailand?

Jones: In those days, we had Air Force people in South Vietnam and a bunch of other bases. We also had bases in Thailand. There were 4 or 5 bases in Thailand and my squadron was deployed to Ubon. We flew over in July of 1967 and we joined the 8th Tack Fighter Wing, which was commanded by Colonel Robin Olds, who was also a West Point graduate. He was an Ace in WWII and was, in my opinion, the best pilot I ever saw. He was our leader and our mission over there was to fly missions and deliver ordinance and things in North Vietnam. We flew some missions in Laos also, but you had to have 100 missions over North Vietnam to go home, or one year. To fly the 100 missions would normally take 8 or 9 months or so.

Throneberry: Tell us what happened on January 18, 1968.

Jones: We took off on a mission, it was a power plant. We were dropping a new weapon that was called a "Walleye." It was a TV glide bomb. It had a TV camera in the nose of the bomb. It had little wings on it so you would roll in and you had a little TV camera in our picture tube in the cockpit. You roll in on the target, lock it on and you could release the weapon and it could fly down to the target by itself. They were very expensive. At that time they were $50,000 or $100,000 apiccc. To drop iron bombs like the rest of the time we did, it would take many, many of those to destroy a target that one of these would destroy. Four of us had these weapons. We rolled in and dropped the weapons and as we pulled off, the airplane was hit almost immediately. The airplane started coming apart, the nose came off and it pitched forward and the controls didn't work anymore.

There wasn't much else to do but eject. There were 2 of us in the airplane so both of us ejected and we were out 6, 7 or 8,000 feet and you are in a little bit of shock now coming down. I remember looking down and all I saw was water. We had a sea kit that was attached to us which had a one-man life raft so I deployed the sea kit, so I'm ready for a water landing. As we came down, this was a very populated area and we could hear cheering, then a few shots coming up from the parachutes. So a few of them were shooting at us, and I was coming down lower and lower, I landed in this rice patty and it was a water landing but the water was only 1 ½ feet deep.

We ran together and there was nowhere to go and nowhere to hide. Immediately we were surrounded by a huge mob of Vietnamese. They were more like a militia. Some had uniforms, some had hats, but they all had weapons. Every person had a gun, knife, sharp stick, sharp stones. There were little kids and old people and obviously, they are not happy because we just bombed everything.

Unfortunately, there was a lot of MIAs. A lot of guys probably didn't make it because you're not in control of any regular military yet.

Jones: So, we were surrounded and an old man came out of the crowd who seemed the village chief and he wanted our weapons. We carried a side arm. We emptied our guns, threw them in a rice patty and broke our radios. Once we did that, the mass of humanity descended on us and it was a tough time. Everyone wants to show you their weapon and hit or beat you. They took our flight suits, cut our boots off and left us standing in our underwear.

Throneberry: They pretended they were going to shoot you?

Jones: All of the sudden they moved everyone away from us and they had us sitting on an embankment, all tied up, everyone was in front of us and I looked up and there were 6-8 young Vietnamese and they were lined up. My compatriot, Bruce Hinkley, turned around and said they were going to shoot us. Fortunately, for us, the old guy came out of the crowd and was arguing with these young people. We couldn't understand what they were saying. Fortunately, the old guy won the argument, we got rounded up and after we got drug through a couple villages that night with hate rallies. We went into Hanoi that night, into the Hanoi Hilton, which was the nickname of the prison. Bruce went one way and I went the other and I didn't see him for 5 years.

Throneberry: Did they throw you in solitary?

Jones: A little portion of the Hanoi Hilton was called "Heartbreak Hotel" and this is where most of the new POWs were put. It was an old French prison and there were 8 cells in a little tiny cell block and the rooms were 7' x 7', about 12' ceiling and there were concrete bunks formed right on the side of the walls and a heavy wooden door with a flap that they could push down and look in on you. It had an open barred window up high on the wall and there was a lone light bulb hanging on a wire. The walls were 18" thick with drain holes on the bottom. On the bunks were built-in stocks. They put me in the stocks and closed the stocks and I'm still handcuffed and everything. They just left me. The first thing I noticed is there were 4 or 5 rats running in and out of the room.

Throneberry: How long were you kept in that cell?

Jones: I was in that cell for probably a couple of days. It was cold because it was in January. Believe it or not, Vietnam in the winter got cold, and I was freezing. I remember looking down at my legs and they were black and my feet were black, and I thought I got dirty. Then I shook my head and it really wasn't dirt, they were covered with mosquitos and bugs. Fortunately, at that time, I couldn't feel anything. Eventually they came and took me into interrogation. We, of course, had been to survival school and being from a military school, we had some training on this and what to expect.

According to a Geneva Convention, we were only required, as prisoners of war, to give name, rank, serial number and date of birth, but the Vietnamese didn't recognize the Geneva Convention so they would say "You are not a prisoner of war, you are the blackest criminal in the Democratic Republic of Vietnam." And I remember saying to the interrogator one time, "the Democratic Republic of Vietnam, you mean North Vietnam?" He had his 2 guards beat me up because he said "Vietnam is one, there is no north, there is no south."

All us were beaten and tortured to a certain degree. I was a First Lieutenant. I was 24 years old and I didn't know any national secrets or anything that I could tell them, if I wanted to. You soon learn that they can defeat you pretty easily physically. Mentally, it was a different story because you had to stay strong mentally. You didn't want them to do to you what they just did a few times more. I went through that heavy torture 3 more times. Eventually, they wanted to know where you were from, where's your home town, what's your parent's name. Who were you flying with that day?

There were 2 answers they wouldn't take. One was "I won't tell you" and the other was "I don't know." You had to come up with something. You're afraid here a little bit because maybe the next time you go in, they are going to ask you the same question, so you better have the same answer. So, I was flying with the New York Yankees, I was flying with Yogi Berra, Mickey Mantle, Roger Marris, Nelson Howard and so they accepted that, no problem. It was really just a drill with them. They knew we didn't know anything, they just wanted to prove to us, "look, we're the boss and we are telling you what to do."

Throneberry: How often did you mix in with other prisoners?

Jones: I was in solitary for 8 or 9 weeks. If they could have kept us alone, they would have the whole time, but so many people were shot down that logistically, they just couldn't do it. I had a roommate after 8 or 9 weeks, then I was moved into a room with 4 people and then eventually to a room with 9. At that time, 9 of us, we were all kind of segregated by rank, all lieutenants, all junior people. Some of the senior people like Edwin Stockdale, Colonel Reisner, they were lieutenant colonels when they were shot down or commanders in the Navy. The Vietnamese were not stupid. They knew that to keep the senior people segregated from the junior people was what they wanted. Stockdale was in solitary confinement for over 4 years. You are different when you come out of something like that.

Throneberry: Your military training seemed to kick in because when you said you were in these cells with additional people, you sort of set up a command chain and everybody had their jobs.

Jones: We all went to survivor school, whether it was Navy or Air Force. We set up a military chain in each room and the senior guy was called the SRO (senior ranking officer) and he set up the room how he wanted to do it. Our senior guy was an Air Force Lieutenant. He had an operations officer, supply officer, etc., and I always seemed to be the lowest ranking and the youngest. One day he said to me "Bob, in a squadron, you usually have the officers and the men. You're the men."

Throneberry: I don't want to go through all of the torture that you've gone through, but I would like you to tell our audience as it got closer, how did you survive that 5 years?

Jones: We just really went day-by-day. After you are there for a while, it seems like the minutes and hours and days kind of went slowly but, believe it or not, the months and the years seemed to pass quickly. Later on, they put us in bigger rooms because they had an attempted rescue, the Son Tay Raid, the Vietnamese were afraid that the Americans were going to come right downtown and get everybody. They moved us all back into Hanoi. We had lived in about 5 different camps spread out all over the Hanoi area but we all moved back into the Hanoi Hilton and we lived in rooms that were about 40' x 20' and there were 56 of us in that room.

We were pretty tight, but we were happy because we were all together. We became very organized in these rooms. There were some smart guys. We had some classes. This was done somewhat semi-covertly because the Vietnamese weren't sanctioning any of these things. We had classes in Spanish and Literature, so guys came home and got college credits for some of these classes.

We had a regimen every day. We would try to exercise. It was kind of a snowball thing. If you exercised, you tried to stay a little healthier and then you could eat the food they gave you. The food varied from horrible to bad and from bad to horrible. It was pretty much the same every day, 2 meals a day and mostly some kind of soup, maybe some rice and bread.

Throneberry: As your time in Hanoi seems to be lengthening, you are hearing things about the peace talks and so forth.

Jones: In every room there was a loud speaker we called "Hanoi Hannah" so you got mostly propaganda, but once in a while, you would get some real stuff. We heard the Paris talks were going on and finally, one day we were called out and the camp commander had us all stand at ranks. This was the first time they ever treated us like a military organization. Before that, we were criminals. We were told year after year, "We will try you, we will convict you, we will execute you, you will never go home." We didn't believe that. Finally, in early 1973, they took us out and read us the Paris agreements. And, of course, Henry Kissinger had been over there, and they had come to this agreement that if the Americans would pull out of South Vietnam over a time period, then they would release us. We were released in 4 separate groups and going home in order of shoot down. I was shot down in January 1968, but there were guys that were there for 3 years before me. McCain was shot down in 1967. The first guy was shot down in August 1964.

31

Throneberry: Did they fatten you up before they let you go?

Jones: No, not at all. We were hungry all the time. The Hanoi Hilton commander died in 1969 and he was a nasty guy. Our treatment changed gradually after he died. On the day we left, we had "weed soup." We just got more food, so we weren't as hungry. If they had let us go in 1968 or 1969, we would have looked a lot different. We were a little skinny when we came home, but we usually had enough food to be full, but I had enough soup and enough rice. Believe it or not, I still like rice. I don't like weed soup.

Throneberry: Tell me about your first meal.

Jones: They took us to Clark Air Force Base in the Philippines and were taken into the hospital. We went downstairs into the cafeteria and they had a big buffet line set up. I was in the third group to come home, so the first group had already been there and the second group also. So, they had determined what the menu was going to be, it was steak and eggs, so I remember going down the line and filling up with steak and eggs and ate the whole thing on the way, and just turned around and went right back in line again.

Throneberry: Tell me about your civilian life. You did not stay in the Air Force?

Jones: I stayed in for 3 years. I resigned from the Air Force. I flew with American Airlines for 27 years. I've retired from American.

CHAPTER 3
LEFT FOR DEAD

It was almost 2100 hrs on 29 January 1968, the night before the "Tet Offensive" when Wendell Skinner's helicopter crashed in Cambodia attempting to extract a Special Forces (SF) Long Range Patrol Team that had come in contact with a large force of Viet Cong and NVA.

The Landing Zone (LZ) was a burned out area in the jungle that was covered with ashes. As the helicopter made its approach the ashes flew up around the aircraft blinding the pilot and he made a hard landing resulting in the pilot being thrown through the windshield still strapped in his seat almost tearing his arm off. The co-pilot and door gunner were thrown against the dash and suffered broken bones.

Skinner was thrown under the Huey as it rolled over and started to burn. Thinking Skinner was dead, another Huey picked up the wounded crew and the SF Team and left the area leaving Skinner.

Major Earl Carson, CO of the 195th Assault Helicopter Company was awakened shortly after midnight and told of the crash and the loss of Skinner. Carlson was outraged. "You don't leave a soldier, dead or alive, behind." He had never lost a man under his command. He gathered a crew together and went to find Skinner. "I was just doing what a commanding officer is supposed to do."

September 25, 2010

Throneberry: We are going to talk about an incident that happened in 1968. This is about a helicopter crewman who crashed and was left out in the field. We are going to go back in time to the 29th of January, 1968, the night before the Tet Offensive occurred. Tell me about the mission you were on and what happened.

Wendell Skinner: We had several teams out along the Ho Chi Minh Trail. We were watching a movie and just as the movie ended, the siren went off. If I remember correctly, we didn't even have anyone go to the operations tent to get the coordinates. We just got on the chopper. It was me, Frank Miller, Woody Woodworth who was my pilot, and Tom Campbell who was my co-pilot. We took off and Woody was hitting the coordinates as we were flying to the side.

As we were going to the side, we also got in contact with the team and they were whispering on the radio which meant that VC was right on top of them. They told us they were putting deep back in the jungle and they were trying to get back to the LZ. They had a blue strobe light and they would hit that thing just to let us know where we were at. We were just flying in a circle to wait until they told us to come in.

When we got the word to come in, I remember we were taking a little bit of fire and there was so much going on. I looked up to Woody to say something and all of this stuff came flying over the windshield. The next thing I know, I'm lying in a bunch of wires and I had no clue what had happened. What happened is that area had just been burned out. Woody's recollection was that he had lost contact with the ground. He thought he was close to setting down that he just cut power and bam – we hit real hard.

He went flying out of the front windshield and his one arm almost got torn off. I was laying underneath the helicopter and not knowing what was going on. I kept waking up and then passing out and hearing all this chatter outside. I kept hearing the gunship flying around and circling. Then all of the sudden, the chatter stopped and then I heard the slow wind of the chopper motor winding up and then the helicopter took off. Then about 5 or 6 hours passed. All I could think of was if the VC come inside the chopper and find me all torn up, they would just shoot me.

Throneberry: Your leg was hurt pretty bad?

Skinner: I was pinned under the helicopter sitting in an upright position. My knee and thigh were completely crushed by the helicopter. Believe it or not, I wasn't feeling any pain. I never heard Major Carlson's helicopter come up because I was in and out of consciousness. Then someone came up into the chopper and looked down at me and said "Huh, we thought you were dead." I remember being put on the evac helicopter which Major Carlson was flying and going to the 930 evacuation hospital. When I woke up the next morning I was in a ward of amputees. I thought, I'm not looking.

The doctor came in and I asked "Am I in one piece?" He said "Yes, but you will never walk right again." From there, I went to Japan and then ended up at Valley Forge VA Hospital for a year.

Throneberry: I want to go back to the night you were shot down or crashed. I want you to imagine you are driving in a fog and you can't see the ground and you suddenly stop 10 feet short of where you wanted to be and then let it coast forward and crash into the wall. That is similar to what happened. I'm sure Woody got a little vertigo and wasn't sure what was up and what was down and thought he was close to the ground and would land because of all of the ash flying around. He brings it in hard and the pilot goes out the windshield, seat and all. There was a lot of panic and concern on the ground because you not only had a helicopter hit the ground and roll over, you had Special Forces trying to get everybody out and get them on one helicopter because they were getting shot at at the same time.

Skinner: Woody and I were talking about this the other night and we had a belly man that went out with us. He was actually a pilot that wanted to come along and experience a night extraction. We think that when they found him, it was me. In the meantime, Woody got out of his seat and he heard me screaming and he was trying to dig me out. Then he passed out from loss of blood. It was pitch black and I'm not sure if these guys had flashlights. Another thing, where we were at was a big buildup of the Tet Offensive in that area and I'm sure that the VC did not want to compromise their position by coming in there and just killing everybody.

Throneberry: Major Carlson, tell me what happened around midnight that night.

Carlson: From my unit, we had half a dozen aircraft up to a place called Long Bay Mound. It was a place off the peak of a mountain and the Special Forces camped there. That is where we went. I put all our people up there on a 2 minute notice. You sleep by your aircraft and as soon as the first mortar comes, if the enemy should choose to take us, within 2 minutes I expected every aircraft to be airborne. We knew that there were tens of thousands of people coming through the jungle down south toward Saigon.

I felt that we might be attacked at any time but that we were going to make them pay a price for it. The night before Tet, in the afternoon before, we got a call back to Saigon where the helicopters were meeting the Special Forces there. That night I was sleeping and after midnight this kid woke me up and told me we had lost an aircraft.

We had some pretty good battles at that point, but hadn't had any loss of life or aircraft. One of my questions was did we get all of our crew back? He said "Yeah, we got everybody but one who was trapped underneath the aircraft and left for dead." I thought, the first order of battle among soldiers is you never leave your people for dead. I was furious with the pilot and co-pilot that they would go off and leave him there. What I didn't find out until a year ago, the pilot and co-pilot and the other member of the ship were as bad as he was and I couldn't understand that they were passing out from time to time just like Wendell was. It was a terrible scene there.

I got a co-pilot and got up in my chopper and went to the scene. It was a full moon and the trees had been burned out. The ground was covered with ashes. It was like something out of a Boris Karloff movie, like a ghost scene. It was pretty obvious to me as we were coming in that we were going to be flying blind and I told the co-pilot to watch carefully what I do and get your mind set on where you are and what your rate of descent is so that you can get down to the ground and you are not going to have a lot of road on the aircraft so you won't have to worry about stalling out and crashing. I'm going to get out and bring back Wendell. We made a really good landing there and I was surprised because we were blind for about the last 50 feet going in.

Of course, we were risking another aircraft and crew but we often take chances in combat and you do what you have to do. I was sure I heard this loud piercing scream that made my hair stand up and I recognized that he was out there and still alive. So I got the crew chief and we piled out of the aircraft and I told the co-pilot to take it up and wait for a call. We also recognized there could have been anywhere between 10-20,000 NVA (North Vietnamese Army) out there. We got a hold of the tail section of the aircraft and far enough for Wendell to slide out from underneath the aircraft. I called my co-pilot to bring it in and we got all we could off the aircraft and took Wendell back. Wendell may not know this but they came out the next morning with the helicopter wrecker crew and lifted it out of there and took it back to salvage.

Throneberry: So you got Wendell out?

Carlson: Yes, I took him to the medevac hospital that was not very far from our base.

Throneberry: Wendell, you were sent to a medevac hospital and then Major Carlson had to deal with another project the next day around 3am. Can you tell me about that?

Skinner: I was actually in the hospital the next day when the Tet offensive hit and I think they overran the air base at one time and they came and got all of the patients and put us in a bunker with no weapons and nobody was there with us and I thought, if they get in here, it's going to be a mass slaughter.

Skinner: I will say something about Woody, he talks about this every time we talk. He has a lot of guilt about the way things went. He lost sight of the ground. I'm sure he has a lot of problems thinking it was his fault that everybody got screwed up. I never once had a problem with what he did. Like the Major said, when you are in combat, there is a certain amount of chaos and Woody did what he thought he should do.

Throneberry: Wendell had been shot down and the aircraft rolled over on him and Major Carlson had gone out in the middle of the night and got him out of there. They just met up with each other last year after almost 42 years. Major Carlson, I wanted to ask you about the Tet. When they did over run Bien Hoa and Long Binh, how long were they able to hold the land and were we able to fight them off at the time?

Carlson: Long Binh was oriented as a north and south base and we were on the west side of that airfield. They had an evacuation hospital about ½ or ¾ of a mile, it was nothing but brush and underbrush and little hills. At 3am, all hell broke loose. The mortars started going off and machine gun fire everywhere. I was afraid we were going to run out of ammunition because our communication wires had been cut and we lost contact. They were shooting at us and I told the men that if they see something out there, just don't waste the ammunition. They said they saw a couple guys jump up there and we opened fire and then we got a lot of fire back. What I surmised was that a couple of these kids walked in there, one had a pink shirt on and one had a blue shirt on, and they were jumping up to draw fire. Then the fire was going to the hospital and the hospital was firing back with us. I radioed the hospital and told them to please stop firing for 15 minutes and I would do the same so we can see what is causing this. Then it was complete silence. I wasn't sure if that was the same hospital I took Wendell to or not. Then there was this big explosion that rattled the windows and building. Everyone hit the floor. I jumped up and ran across the bodies and got outside just in time to see a nuclear weapon cloud go up. I thought, here we are surrounded, we have no chance of getting out of here, we are going to be outnumbered and they are giving up on us. Then I found out about 2 hours later, a million gallon tank of JP4 had been set off by choppers and that is what I saw.

Throneberry: Any last words?

Skinner: I'm just thrilled I got this story out there and soon I'm going to see Major Carlson and give him a big hug because without his efforts, I would not be here today.

Carlson: I would like to say this, for all the guys and particularly the young men who were drafted in our unit, that first mission we had, that was a scary night. A lot of young boys became men. It was one heck of a site and from there on out, we were solid.

CHAPTER 4
TET OFFENSIVE

"The Tet Offensive was one of the largest military campaigns of the Vietnam War, launched on January 30, 1968 by forces of the Viet Cong and North Vietnamese Army against the forces of South Vietnam, the United States, and their allies. It was a campaign of surprise attacks against military and civilian commands and control centers throughout South Vietnam.

The communists launched a wave of attacks in the late night hours of 30 January in the I and II Corps Tactical Zones of South Vietnam. This early attack did not lead to widespread defensive measures. When the main communist operation began the next morning the offensive was countrywide and well-coordinated, eventually more than 80,000 communist troops striking more than 100 towns and cities, including 36 of 44 provincial capitals, five of the six autonomous cities, 72 of 245 district towns, and the southern capital. The offensive was the largest military operation conducted by either side up to that point in the war.

The initial attacks stunned the US and South Vietnamese armies and caused them to temporarily lose control of several cities, but they quickly regrouped to beat back the attacks, inflicting massive casualties on communist forces.

During the Battle of Hue, intense fighting lasted for a month resulting in the destruction of the city by US forces. During their occupation, the communists executed thousands of people in the Massacre at Hue. Around the US combat base at Khe Sanh fighting continued for two more months.

Although the offensive was a military defeat for the communists, it had a profound effect on the US government and shocked the US public, which had been led to believe by its political and military leaders that the communists were, due to previous defeats, incapable of launching such a massive effort.

The term "Tet offensive" usually refers to the January–February 1968 offensive, but it can also include the so-called "Mini-Tet" offensives that took place in May and August."

General James H. Willbanks had a distinguished military career and academic career. He retired from the Army with twenty-three years' service as an Infantry officer in various assignments, to include a tour as an advisor with a South Vietnamese regiment during the 1972 North Vietnamese Easter Offensive. He holds a B.A. in History from Texas A&M University, and an M.A. and Ph.D. in History from the University of Kansas. He was the George C. Marshall Chair of Military History and Director of the Department of Military History at the U.S. Army Command and General Staff College, Fort Leavenworth, Kansas. He is the author or editor of fifteen books, including A Raid Too Far (Texas A&M University Press),

Abandoning Vietnam (University Press of Kansas), The Battle of An Loc (Indiana University Press), and The Tet Offensive: A Concise History (Columbia University Press.

February 2, 2013

Throneberry: Tell our audience about the Tet Offensive and the planning and so forth that led up to it.

General Willbanks: The planning for the Tet Offensive began in 1967. The planning started in Hanoi and there was some discussion among the Viet Cong and the North Vietnamese. There were two factions within the politburo. One faction wanted to go for an all-out attack. The other faction was to continue the protracted warfare approach and in the end those who were proponents for the all-out attack won the argument and that resulted in the Tet Offensive.

Throneberry: The NV overall commander didn't necessarily want to have this Tet Offensive the way the politburo wanted it, is that correct?

General Willbanks: Actually, the proponent was another general in the south, Central Office for South Vietnam. He and one of the other leaders in the politburo were the proponents for the all-out attack. Others counseled to be a little bit more cautious and continue with the protracted approach.

Throneberry: Early in 1967, the North Vietnamese decided that they needed to do this major offensive. What were the purposes of this?

General Willbanks: Those who were proponents of it clearly believed that it could be a war winning strategy. The only way they convinced themselves of that was to couple the attack with a general uprising by the people of South Vietnam. Otherwise, it didn't make much sense militarily because if you looked at the combat ratios, South Vietnamese and the other free world military forces clearly outnumbered the other side in the south particularly in terms of fire power. There are some people in the south who have been fighting the Americans and the South Vietnamese who are questioning the idea of going forward with such a large scale attack and they're basically accused of subjective thinking and told, essentially, to keep rolling. So, once they've convinced themselves that this is going to work, then it takes on a new life of itself and ultimately 80,000 enemy soldiers are involved.

Throneberry: How did they get all of these soldiers and supplies into South Vietnam?

General Willbanks: They had been going down the Ho Chi Minh Trail in the early 1960s. Initially, at the end of the first China War, they left somewhere between 5,000 and 10,000 cavalry in the south that became what we call Viet Cong and they were strengthening those forces. After late 1964, the North Vietnamese main force moved into South Vietnam. We were never able to cut the Ho Chi

Minh Trail, so it continued to be a line of supply for the North Vietnamese throughout the war.

Throneberry: For our civilian audiences, we should point out that the Ho Chi Minh Trail came down from North Vietnam, ran through Laos and Cambodia, before it entered back into South Vietnam. Due to, I guess, political reasons, we were not allowed to go into Laos and Cambodia and to just destroy the trail, is that correct?

General Willbanks: With two exceptions. In 1970, Nixon sent US and South Vietnamese forces into Cambodia. A very disruptive raid that took many out in the base camps and sanctuaries in Cambodia. And then in 1971, about 20,000 South Vietnamese forces went down Highway 9 from Khe Sanh into Laos to attack that part of the Ho Chi Minh Trail. US forces were not permitted on the ground because of congressional legislation but we supported it with massive amounts of air support, helicopters and artillery firing from within South Vietnam into Laos. The bottom line was if you could not occupy the Ho Chi Minh Trail, then it was very difficult to cut off supplies. We bombed it for essentially the length of the entire war but were never really able to cut it off.

Throneberry: The unit that I worked with would go into Cambodia and do things that they were not supposed to talk about and I'm still not supposed to talk about it, I guess. To try to disrupt the trail and all these other things, they would say that the bombings would come through, the trail would be destroyed, and before the morning they had rebuilt it again.

General Willbanks: The problem was, it really wasn't a trail, it was more like a capillary system so there might be 3 or 4 laterals running north to south and you could take out one with a B52 strike and basically they could move over 1500 meters and keep moving south. Meanwhile, after the bombing was over, they had a large amount of troops that were there just to maintain and secure the trail. They would go back and repair the trail. So our guys who were bombing the trail, bombed the same places over and over again. If you couldn't send troops in there to essentially clean out the sanctuaries, then the war sustains itself forever. That was always one of the problems. We were fighting a limited war, they were fighting a total war.

Throneberry: In the book, there were 3 main objectives. The first was to cause this big uprising and hopefully get the South Vietnamese to fall. What were the other ones?

General Willbanks: Essentially, the fall of the Saigon government was the ultimate prize. The unstated one, or at least the ancillary reason, would be to demonstrate to the US that the war was not winnable. In a sense, they do achieve that, at least to a large part of the American public. So despite the fact that they are defeated soundly during the fighting, which, by the way, extends up into the Fall, that was really 3 phases. The one that gets the popular conception is of the early fighting in 1968 but the fighting does continue up into the end of September or early part of October and they lose over 40,000 troops. I got to Vietnam in 1971 and I never saw Viet Cong because militarily where I was, they had been wiped out in 1968.

Throneberry: I got there in 1969, and they were still there, but not in as great of numbers as they had been in the previous part of that. Can you talk a little about the attack on the Base of Khe Sanh?

General Willbanks: There was a big North Vietnamese build up beginning at the end of 1967 and the first couple of weeks of January 1968. This drew everyone's attention primarily because, in Khe Sanh, when you look at it on a map, it looks a lot like the Dien Bien Phu. It's out at a long line of communication up against the Laos ocean border so there were many parallels that were drawn in the media as well as in the White House between Khe Sanh and the Dien Bien Phu. General William Westmoreland thought that was where the main attack was going to come from. He continued to believe that even in the first week of the Tet Offensive. There was a lot of discussion in history about what was going on in there. It looks like it was a great misdirection played to focus everyone's attention away from the populated areas, which would be the focus of the Tet Offensive. But, essentially, 20,000 North Vietnamese surrounded Khe Sanh. The difference between Khe Sanh and the Dien Bien Phu is that rather than like the French who stayed down in the low ground, the Marines occupied the high ground that surrounded Khe

Sanh and there were lots of sharp fighting there. That was the biggest battle in town. The initial shelling began, if I remember right, began on January 21, so fully about 9 or 10 days before the main attack came.

Throneberry: The North Vietnamese also were having all these little probing attacks up and down Vietnam, weren't they?

General Willbanks: They had done that all along. They had prepared the battlefield pretty well in 1967. There had been a number of battles: the Siege of the Marines on Kantian on the DMZ, the earlier fights around Khe Sanh which were known as the "Hill Fights", battles at Song Bay and locked in up against the Cambodian border, Military Region 3, and then a giant battle in November at Dak To. These were what we would call today and Army doctrine shaping operation, meant to pull the focus of the American high command away from populated centers. Put these on a map, these are along the DMZ and along the Laos and Cambodian borders. So there was a wholesale repositioning of US forces to respond to these actions. Essentially, by the time of Khe Sanh, you've got a large percentage of the US forces are located in I Corps in response to these movements in the buildup in Khe Sanh.

Throneberry: That was obviously a major battle and many of us are very familiar with the battle for Khe Sanh.

One of the things that I read, when they were attacking Khe Sanh, they were just showering it with artillery and mortars and everything else, they did hit a supply of CS tear gas.

General Willbanks: Essentially, they hit the ammo dump and then the ammo dump was CS tear gas which I'm sure made it uncomfortable for the Marines until it dissipated.

Throneberry: I landed one time in LZ that somebody had said was marked with white smoke. And I was asking, what is white smoke? We've never seen white smoke before and as we got closer, we found out it was a CS grenade that somebody had thrown out.

On January 31, 1968, a Tet Offensive occurred. Where did it happen and what happened on that night?

Willbanks. It actually started out on the 30th. It was supposed to start on the 31st. There were targets that ranged from the DMZ to the tip of the Peninsula. They were all populated areas and 23 bases and installations including a number in Saigon, Da Nang and other larger cities. The reason that there was an earlier attack in an area localized essentially around the southern part of I Corps and the northern part of II Corps, it turned out that the forces were using 2 separate lunar calendars that were off by 24 hours. Now that gave the American troops some alert that something was coming because the attacks started 24 hours early. It didn't help the ARVN (Army of Republic of Vietnam or South Vietnam Army) much because this was a Tet holiday and a large part of the ARVN forces were home on leave so they couldn't be recalled in 24 hours. Then the offensive launched its full fury on the 31st up and down the length of Vietnam. General Frederick Weyand said that the situation map lit up like a pinball machine. All the attacks were ongoing.

Throneberry: Joining me now is Mike Mullins. Now I'm going to put you on hold and go back to Colonel Willbanks. The attacks occurred the evening of Tet. All the South Vietnamese are technically off on a break. It's a very big religious holiday. Back in your book I read something about 1789, that the Vietnamese did the same thing to the Chinese?

Willbanks. That is correct. You have decided that the other side is on the ropes so if you get indication that they are not on the ropes, you just discounted as a false report. Then, of course, if there is a build up at Khe Sanh, which happened in the early part of 1968, if you begin to see that maybe something is in the works, then what that something is, is Khe Sanh. Then when the attack breaks in all its fury from north to south on January 30 and 31, it's totally unexpected.

Throneberry: The motivation for this program today is that, obviously, it is the anniversary of Tet, but also because I read in a magazine called "Vietnam" and it had some great articles in there and talked about how the troops were being moved all over the country to put out these fires in various places and then Saigon was attacked. How could the North Vietnamese and the Viet Cong get into the American Embassy?

General Willbanks: Saigon is really only 65 miles away from the Cambodian border. It's a pretty easy run from the sanctuaries in Cambodia to Saigon. They began moving those forces in the late 1967 toward Saigon. Of course a lot of the forces that were used inside the cities particularly Saigon were Viet Cong units not North Vietnamese. It's kind of interesting because General Frederick Weyand, who commanded the 25th infantry division and then went on to be the Air Force Commander, thought that something was up. He began to reposition some of his forces closer to Saigon because Saigon essentially was left to the South Vietnamese to defend. We didn't have any combat troops in Saigon. He moved a couple of his battalions, one of his cavalry outfits, a little closer, and those are the guys that responded once the fighting started in Saigon, they and the ARVN who were located in the area. That turned out to be a success story and, of course all those troops that were seized in Saigon, they were all killed or captured including the sappers (commandos) inside the grounds of the Embassy. They never actually made it in. I think they made it to the bottom floor but never above the ground floor and they were all killed or captured.

Throneberry: The story of the attack on Saigon was what so many people heard about here in the States and that is where I want to make this transition now to what was the story we were hearing here at home? And you talk about that being one of the objectives of this

Tet Offensive. That the North Vietnamese wanted the American people to know that things were not going quite as smoothly as we thought.

General Willbanks: I think that was one of the objectives to show that the war was going to continue. It wasn't going to be over as Westmoreland said. In November he had said that in 2 years we would have it under control. They were more than happy to prove that that wasn't the case. You make a very good point about the fighting in Saigon because that is what is readily available to the news media. There were 636 media personnel who were accredited in Saigon on January 31, 1968. Some of those were very good like Joe Galloway and some were not very experienced so what you got was their perception of the war and you didn't have to go anywhere. Those very splashy pictures and those very splashy videos are what is on the news at 5:30 every night. The nature of the media is such that you don't go to page 13 for the rest of the story. The rest of the story in the Embassy fight is, they are all dead or captured. What you see is the fact that you have 19 sappers inside the grounds of the US Embassy, the seat of power in Vietnam, those were pretty powerful images.

Throneberry: Mike, I want you to jump in on this. The reason I asked you to be on today is because you had written an article a long time ago when you were starting to work on one of your books about newsman Walter Cronkite. Everybody trusted this man and we thought that he would only give us the truth and he made a line that the war had been lost, and I will let you go on that, Mike.

Mullins: That was a major turning point. Most of us who served in the field, served in Vietnam. I got there in March. I was a replacement basically for the 199th, which was heavily engaged in a hotel race track in Cholon.

Throneberry: So you were in Saigon?

Mullins: One of the primary duties of the 199th had been that they intercepted the NVA (North Vietnam Army or People's Army of Vietnam) moving in from the northwest prior to the main attack. Several battalions as well as the 199th were airlifted into Cholon to take the race track back. The race track was the central point because there were five roads converged there.

Throneberry: Mike you were with the 199th and were at the race track?

Mullins: The 199th took the race track back from the VC (Viet Cong). That was a key intersection for them for moving troops in and heavier armor and things. When I got there in March, the guys who brought me in had survived a lot that. They fought at Long Binh. They fought a Camp Frenzell-Jones, which is the main base camp for the 199th and then fought at Cholon. The prospective when you brought up Cronkite, there were many of us who resent the fact that he told the world we were losers when, in fact, we kicked the enemy out of that area. In fact, we ran them out of the country. It was one of those things that we felt it was somebody we had trusted, and we were kids, and we didn't know how seriously it was going to impact the people at home. To tell the American public based on what he saw in a few blocks rather than getting after-battle reports to see how we really faired. He made an assumption and announced how bad it was and how badly we were doing in the middle of a fight. There was a lot of underlying anger and resentment by a lot of guys who fought there and went there right after.

Throneberry: I would think it would hurt recruiting and so forth, it certainly played with our minds, what are we doing there if we aren't going to win?

General Willbanks: I think you can look at a couple of polls that are very instructive. If you look at November 1967, 50% of those who took the poll thought the US was making progress in Vietnam. In February 1968, after the Tet Offensive hit, 61% thought that we were losing or standing still. So I think the impact of the Tet Offensive was extremely large and went a long way if you were against the war, it certainly cemented those feelings. If you were on the fence it, perhaps, pushed you in the other direction. Even if you were to give the President Lyndon Johnson administration the benefit of the doubt based upon what they had told you in late 1967, the images on TV, right or wrong, sort of said a different story.

Throneberry: Mike, any comments on that?

Mullins: The soldiers didn't lose it. The politicians and the press did. We lost that war. There was no peace with honor. The fighting that was done was never reported in a positive light. The information that was going home to the American public was that we were a bunch of losers and we had a bad battle plan. I'm not so sure they weren't accurate in that part. There were a lot of people who saw it coming and were prepared. Nothing they intended to overrun was overrun. Their supply lines were completely destroyed and Viet Cong was almost completely destroyed. If we had been allowed to chase them back into the hole where they went, we could have dealt a serious blow to the North Vietnamese. So the limitations placed on us, the press should have been reporting not on our performance in the battlefield but how our performance was being restricted. In most of our minds, or many of the people I know that I've communicated with over the years were absolutely convinced that the press lost that and everybody that came thereafter, later in 1968 and up into 1969, thought they were coming to a losing effort. It's almost like a kid on the playground, the last one chosen knows he is going to a losing team and really would rather go home. The emotional impact of those reports coming home and then what we heard from home while we were in the field trying to do our thing was a total disaster morale wise.

If Ernie Pyle had done what Walter Cronkite did back in WWII, he could have stopped the sale of war bonds.

Throneberry: Going back to Colonel Willbanks, just fill our audience in on what happened to President Johnson after Tet.

General Willbanks: General Wheeler who was the Chairman of the Joint Chiefs convinced General Westmoreland that he should have asked for more troops. So he asked for 206,000 more troops. As you might expect, this doesn't go over very well in an unpopular war that half of America thinks we are losing. At the New Hampshire primary, President Johnson wins by only 300 votes so that convinces him that essentially his political career is over. So on March 31, he goes on national TV and says he will not run, he will not accept his party's nomination and that he will be done at the end of his term. You make a very good point about what is going on the United States, it's a very turbulent one. I was younger at the particular time, I was still in college, and I thought the country was coming apart at the seams. Martin Luther King was assassinated, Bobby Kennedy was assassinated, they had riots in the street at the Democratic National Convention in the Fall and it looked like the whole country was falling apart at the seams.

Throneberry: I know what you mean. I was going through flight training at the time in Texas and we were constantly told that we had to be on alert because Dallas was going to go up in flames over a demonstration over this or whatever happened to be. It was just so frightening to think of what was happening to our country and in my mind, I'm going to go off and fight these bad guys 10,000 miles away, it would be nice if we could straighten these things out here

58

before we do that. And, Mike, I heard you mention that they wouldn't let us finish the job.

Mullins: Exactly. They stopped us. I think that one of the major mistakes was actually predicated in Korea. Taking ground and giving it back.

General Willbanks: Rather than measuring our progress with ground taken and secured, we measured it in body count, and all us resented having to do it in body counts. In April, my unit stumbled into a saber battalion and we whipped them. There were 3 companies in my battalion and one of our units that was flanking us was at the center of the battle and in chasing them down the road, so to speak, they were made to stop and count bodies that were stuffed in a well. The measuring stick that was chosen was a poor way of doing business in my mind. And in our minds at the time, we would rather have won than stopped and counted.

Throneberry: General Willbanks, what lessons do you think we learned from this Tet, if any?

General Willbanks: I think the biggest lesson for the serving military today is to not build unrealistic expectations. I think part of the impact for the Tet Offensive was General Westmoreland saying in November that there was a light at the end of the tunnel, that the war would be over in 2 years. There was still a lot of fighting. I got there in 1971 and the war was still going on. I think that senior leaders have to be really careful about describing the way-ahead. A good example of that was General Petraeus in Iraq at the time of the surge where he was very cautious about saying that there are some hard days ahead. He said some progress is being made, but there are hard days ahead. He was a student of the Vietnam War and I think he realized that the mistakes of Tet were pretty clear and he wasn't going to make those in Iraq.

CHAPTER 5
DEAD MEN FLYING

"Vietnam was a war in which the heroism of the American soldier was accompanied by humanitarianism. The humanitarianism took place during the heat of the battle. The GI fixed as he fought, he cured and educated and built in the middle of the battle. He truly cared for, and about, those people. Humanitarianism was America's great victory in Vietnam. Spearheading the humanitarian efforts were the air ambulance operations, call-sign Dust Off."

This dangerous aviation operation rescued some one million souls in Vietnam. *Dead Men Flying* by General Patrick Brady is the story of Charles Kelly, the father of Dust Off, who gave his life to save Dust Off - the greatest life-saver ever. His dying words – "When I have your wounded" - set the standard for combat medicine to this day.

Veterans Radio's guest was Medal of Honor recipient Major General Patrick Brady, who learned from Charles Kelly and struggled to meet his standard. Brady led the 54th Medical Detachment as it rescued over 21,000 wounded - enemy and friendly - in 10 months.

Major *General Patrick H. Brady* spent over 34 years in the Army serving in stations all over the world. He is one of America's most decorated veterans.

While in Vietnam he was awarded the Medal of Honor for a series of rescues during which he used 3 helicopters to rescue over 60 wounded. At the end of the day, his aircraft had over 400 holes in them from enemy fire and mines. In two tours in Vietnam he flew over 2500 combat missions and personally rescued over 5000 wounded.

Gen. Brady received not only the Medal of Honor but the Distinguished Service Cross, our nation's second highest award. His other awards include two Distinguished Service Medals; the Defense Superior Service Medal; the Legion of Merit; six Distinguished Flying Crosses; two Bronze Stars, one for valor; the Purple Heart and 53 Air Medals, one for valor. He is a member of both the Army Aviation and Dust Off Halls of Fame.

December 1, 2012

Throneberry: You really did live through history, you said you were in Berlin when the Wall went up?

General Brady: Yes. That was my first experience with communism. I was a young idealistic man coming out of college and I had read about Mao Zedong and the Long March and thought, this is a really tough guy, and Russia was in space, and all of the sudden we wake up on August 13 1961, I think it was, and they divided the city of Berlin. As you know, the city was 110 miles behind the Iron Curtain and it was occupied by the four forces. All of the sudden, they are shooting their own people off the Wall. I was a medical platoon leader and we were picking up the mess. And me, being a Second Lieutenant in Berlin, I had a maid and a babysitter. My babysitter's fiancé was in the east at Check Point Charlie in East Germany, she never saw him again. Our maid's mother and father, when they died in the east, she could not go to their funeral. Then, of course, I saw the real horrors of communism in Vietnam and also in Korea when I was working in the DMZ. It was a horrible, evil system. And, of course, that is why I went to Vietnam just to help the helpless people be free of the evils of communism and show them the fruits of freedom. Many GIs did a great job and that is what the book is about – the humanitarian effort over there.

Throneberry: You turned out to be what I used to call an RLO, which was "real life officer." And you had a different name and I'm trying to find it?

General Brady: It was a "RFO" and your listeners can figure that out.

Throneberry: You went to Vietnam for the first time in 1964?

General Brady: Yes. Charles Kelley was one of the greatest heroes I had ever known and he was a veteran of WWII and was severely wounded. He came out, at the time, the only living veteran with all four of the medals. He also had a combat infantry badge and combat medical badge. We didn't know how to use the resource and neither did the leadership.

You have combat going on and the idea was to just protect the Americans. We only had 16,000 Americans in Vietnam when I got there. I wasn't flying a lot so the leadership decided to take it away from Kelley and put a portable Red Cross on it. Kelley said "you are not going to do that, that's insane." Kelley came back and said "listen guys, they don't wish us well. For the first time since the Civil War, they are going to confiscate a medical resource. We have to prove to them that we can do better than they can do." We did our best to keep up with him. We were the only units that flew at night and to fly on the battlefield during the battle. No one else did that. He set incredible records for patient caring. When he would land in a village, the entire village would turn out. And they would say "here are the Americans taking this valuable machine for lives, risking them for a peasant and a rice patty." It made a great impression on the people.

As I tell in the book, the battle went on to take the aircraft away from us and I don't think it was settled until Kelley was killed. He was killed during a pickup, once again on the battlefield, under fire and the people on the ground screamed at him to get out and his dying words were "when I have your wounded." He would not leave until he had their wounded and after he said that, he took a bullet right through the heart. The aircraft died on the spot and General Westmoreland was in charge by then, and they tell me that General Stillwell broke down and cried when he heard that Kelley was dead.

But in any event, that ended it. To this day, his dying words are the standard for Dust Off for medical evacuation across the world.

Throneberry: I think all pilots heard of Kelley in flight school. He was one of those people that was held up as an example that this is what a pilot is supposed to do. We did a lot of ash and trash and did some other stuff working with Special Forces, but we always felt that it was our obligation to help people. We did go in and help people. It didn't make any difference what side they were on and I don't think the American public knew we were doing that.

General Brady: No, and that is one of the great victories of Vietnam. The humanitarian effort over there. For the first time, I think in history, the humanitarian in the midst of this heroic action, the GI also had time for a humanitarian effort. Usually, when we go in, we blow things up, we kill people, civilians or whoever is in our way. In Vietnam we didn't do that. During the battle we fixed, we vaccinated, and we built hospitals and orphanages and adopted those children. Dust Off rescued some 900,000 patients – men, women and children, enemy and well as friendly, even scout dogs when they got hurt. It was a great humanitarian effort. By the way, when I got back, and I've been back 3 times, the people treat me great. The kids in the street especially in Saigon, when I talk to them about America, the place they want to go more than anywhere else is America. We left a great impression on them. They love America to this day and I certainly credit that to the average GI because those people were children now and are grown up now and they've taught their children about how caring the American GI was and how he was there trying to protect them from communism.

Throneberry: Let's go back to Vietnam – 1964/1965. As you mentioned there were only about 16,000 American troops there at the time and the area of operation was everywhere, wasn't it?

General Brady: We covered the entire country with 5 helicopters. We had them located in Saigon and two down in Soc Trang. Initially when I got there, we had one in Pleiku and Quin Yon, covering the north country. Kelley consolidated the two from the north in Soc Trang because that is where the casualties were. His last month, June, before he was killed, he flew 149 hours. The limit was like 90 hours and they tried to stop him by telling him he can't fly that much, it's against regulations. And he said "what do you want me to do, leave the guys in the field?" They didn't mess with him.

Throneberry: They limited us to 120 hours in a 30 day period. They would send you down for a day and you would go back up and start over again. Tell me about when you were in Vietnam the first time, could you describe to us what a typical mission would be and how it operated at that time?

General Brady: We got better later on. In the early days, you get a call. Most often it would come through Vietnamese operations center directly to us at the flight line and we would run to aircraft and had 2 minutes to get off the ground. Very often, in the early days, we had no radio contact with an English speaking person. So we had a set of coordinates heading into the distance and we knew the terrain. We when got there, we would radio "Alpha Bravo" and get back "Charlie Delta" and we know it's friendly. What we would do then is make a very low pass to see if they were friendly or we got shot at. If they looked friendly, we would land. Very often, we had no radio contact. I learned to speak just one mouthful of Vietnamese which was "pop smoke" or "show me your signal" or "show me your address." The smoke could be problematic because if we said they would "pop smoke", they would say if yellow smoke is out, you would look down and you would see two or three yellow smokes. The bad guys would throw it out. After a few bad experiences with that we said "you pop your smoke and I will identify the color." We learned how to make active approaches through trial and error. We would go get the patients and go right to either a Vietnamese or Navy Hospital in south Saigon. At that time, we didn't have a lot of Army or other surgical hospitals or field hospitals. In the early days, we mostly had Vietnamese hospitals. In the north highlands, they wouldn't take mountain yard patients. The first mountain patients, I took into a Vietnamese hospital, I left them on the ramp.

Throneberry: You survived your first tour and what happened when you got back to the states?

General Brady: I went to Fort Benning and we flew in support of the ranger training camp in Florida. At Fort Benning we were flying

H19's, which was really a beast. It actually improved my flying skills because it is difficult to get off the ground. We flew single pilot in those days. All the sudden we got word we were going back to Vietnam and they took everyone out of the unit but me and two other guys. All of the pilots that were going back with us on a second tour had graduated from flight school on the same day. At that time, Dust Off had a good reputation and these guys thought they were handpicked to fly Dust Off. So they took everyone from this class and gave them to me and I had to get them ready to go into combat in a very short time, something like 22 hours. Then we went to Vietnam.

By this time, there were half a million Americans in Vietnam. The first year, we carried 4,000 patients a year. Second tour, we carried almost that many in a month.

We went into a mountain area where the weather and terrain were very difficult. More and more pilots were being killed at night and in the weather, than were killed by the enemy. I was scared to death. I was a hardcore Irish Catholic. My faith is so important. I was praying like crazy to find ways to get the patients out. We found some techniques to help do that and it turned out to be an extraordinary unit and that is the reason I wrote the book.

Throneberry: It was astronomical the amount of patients you were able to save. I'll let you talk about the amount of combat these units saw in Vietnam.

General Brady: I don't think we fought any war where the combat was that intense. The average guy in WWII in 4 years was in combat for 40 days. The average guy in Vietnam in 1 year was in combat about 240 days. I don't think there were soldiers anywhere who had it worse – it was very hot and everything there bit you or stung you. We flew home to an airfield and had sheets on our bed and they were sleeping in the mud. Those guys had it so hard and the way they were treated when they came home was just horrible.

Throneberry: We had another gentleman on the program that talked about tigers in a book called "The Matterhorn." He had talked about losing someone to a tiger.

General Brady: That's true. You have the WIA – wounded in action; KIA – killed in action; EIA – eaten in action. That happened to me in Pleiku where a tiger fell into a fox hole with a guy and mostly ate him before they could get to him. It was dangerous what those guys were doing. Not only because of the enemy who was very proficient in the jungle but because of all of the stuff around them. When I went to Pleiku, they still had plague patients. We would drop these medics out in the villages surrounded by the enemy. They had some exotic diseases out there not to mention hepatitis and some other things.

Throneberry: What made up your crew on a Dust Off aircraft?

General Brady: The crew was a pilot, co-pilot, an aircraft commander who was in charge of the mission. In the back was a medic who was a very highly trained person for treating amputees, gunshot wounds, chest wounds. Then you had the crew chief. He owned the aircraft, it was his job to maintain the aircraft. We had an NCO Sergeant Hodgton who was an absolute genius when it came down to maintenance. We averaged about 4 missions a night. You were looking at a 40 man detachment with 6 aircraft and we covered a monstrous area. Only 3 of them would be flyable at any one time because they were getting shot up. Among those 40 men, 26 received Purple Hearts, that's how many were shot. Some of them were shot more than once, but none of them were killed. In a 9 ½ month period, we carried 21,000 patients. That is more than were carried during the entire Korean War.

Throneberry: Were Dust Off aircrafts armed?

General Brady: Some were, some weren't. The first cav which were not Dust Off, they went by medevac. They were a direct support. We were an area support resource. The first cav actually had the crew chief and the gunner on their aircraft which took up space and didn't do any good. You were authorized to have weapons to protect yourself and your patients. It's hard to teach a guy to shoot out of a helicopter because you actually shoot behind the target. The crew chief and the medic are the gunners when you come into an area, but I didn't want them shooting.

Throneberry: Many of the techniques I read about in your book were things that we were taught once I got in country, not necessarily in flight school.

General Brady: The Medal of Honor and the Distinguished Service Cross, which I have, were a result of two epiphanies I had over there. I was really worried the second tour because we had great challenges in terms of weather.   The first tour I managed a low level fast approach and an overhead of what they called a death spiral, those were routine. The terrain dictated how you got into it. You can't use those approaches in weather especially in the low valley fog and the night tropical storms.

The first technique was a night weather mission. We got a call from Death Valley, it was the middle of a tropical storm and the aircraft was grounded. I headed out and thought I could use techniques from my first tour which was a guy lays on the floor and looks for a light behind you, while you watch for a light in front of you. You go only as far as you see light. Then I had my first epiphany, which I remembered an earlier mission in which I was in the valley, sitting on a mountain top. I looked up and noticed a mountain top and noticed that it was in the clouds that the flares silhouetted it. I went into the weather, flew an IFR to the pickup site and I followed the flares down into the mountains. I made 4 flights that night and got all of the patients out. That solved the night weather problem.

The day weather problems were probably the reason I got the Medal of Honor. The people were on a mountain top watching me come up out of the fog. I got a call one day from a kid who was on a mountain who had been bit by a snake. The clouds went about 500 feet down the mountain top. I got to the mountain, saw clouds and started into it and knew if I got in trouble, I could fall off into the valley. I did that several times. The crew was very nervous and screaming at me that he was going into convulsions. I always flew with my window open and I headed into that stuff one more time. I was blown sideways and that wind was the breadth of God. I looked out my window looking for a hole in the trees. I could see the tip of my rotor blade and the top of the trees. I was right side up and I turned sideways and headed up the mountain and got those guys. The day I got the medal, the fog was at the base of a fire support base and the guys were at the top of the mountain looking down, I would come to a hover at the edge of the clouds, turn it sideways and head in. You could see about 20 feet in that stuff. And that's all you needed to see. If you could see the tip of the rotor blades and the ground or a tree or some other reference point, you can keep it right side up and fly sideways, but not very fast.

General Brady: In the book, I list the awards for that 40 man detachment. It may have been the most highly awarded men ever in terms of awards and medals. You can't always get the guys what they deserve because someone has to see it and care enough to go through the effort to document it. People who did a lot more than I did were never recognized and should have been.

Throneberry: Tell me about what you feel happened as a result of the Vietnam War. The perception is that we lost it. From a military standpoint, that is furthest from the truth, but from a public relations standpoint, we did.

General Brady: The war was lost by the people back here especially the media. The media was the one who demonized the GI when he came home. We all became reclusive and it was until years later that I recognized what a great humanitarian effort it was.

Throneberry: I want to talk about the aircraft. The helicopters have gone from the Apache, Black Hawk and the Huey. In your book you talk about how the Black Hawk cannot do the same thing that a Huey did.

General Brady: The Black Hawk was designed for the aviation mentality. Airfield to airfield. It was not designed to work the jungles. The desert is a different kind of area. I had very little time in the Black Hawk and the Apache, but the Black Hawk has a tail-load attitude. It's not quick, it's powerful and will handle a crash better than a Huey. The Huey is the most combat experienced aircraft in history.

CHAPTER 6
SECRET GREEN BERET COMMANDOS
IN CAMBODIA

Dale Throneberry interviewed Lieutenant Colonel Fred Lindsey (ret) about Military Assistance Command – Studies and Observation Group (MACV-SOG). LTC Fred S. Lindsey, U.S. Army (ret) was the commander of CCS/SOG from Jan-July 1970. His book, A Memorial History of MACV-SOG's Command and Control Detachment South (CCS), and its Air Partners, Republic of Vietnam, 1967-1972, is a definitive history of this very unconventional unit.

10/6/12

Throneberry: Tell me about how the organization got started.

Lindsey: Remember back when the French were fighting the North Vietnamese and they lost that battle? Immediately after that, the Vietnamese starting building what is called the Ho Chi Min Trail. It went down through Cambodia into various parts of South Vietnam. We started putting troops in there as advisors, then 3,500 Marines in Da Nang, but that wasn't until 1965. It was in 1964 that they created Special Observation Group (SOG) to handle all the intelligence gathering in the theater to help the Military Assistance Command – Vietnam (MACV). They handled everything in Thailand, Laos, North Vietnam and Cambodia. They had air

74

operations as well and maritime operations. It was a very slow start, they took over from the CIA when Defense Secretary McNamara wasn't pleased with the results CIA was getting. He came up with a quick plan and was going to have immediate success by creating this organization and they had no one to run it. They started off by grabbing a few Special Forces guys and slowly cobbled it together.

Throneberry: The North Vietnamese had this supply trail that ran from North Vietnam, down through Laos, down through Cambodia and entered into Vietnam at various places along the trail and this is the way they kept resupplying their troops and for some unknown reason, and maybe you can enlighten us on this, we were not allowed to go into Laos and Cambodia and take out this trail.

Lindsey: The Geneva Convention set up Laos and Cambodia as neutral countries and everybody was supposed to stay out of there. But when our people left Laos, I think there were 40 or 50 of our people counted, there were still hundreds of the North Vietnamese in Laos and they stayed there and literally owned the eastern part of it. It was the same thing in Cambodia. The President of Cambodia was not a very good fellow and he made deals with the North Vietnamese to let him come down the trail and he had his own military sort of pulled back about 15 kilometers from the border so they didn't interfere with one another, so they pretty much had free reign to go back and forth behind that border.

Lindsey: The SOG didn't get operational until 1966 when the fifth Special Forces group, which was not a part of SOG, they handled all the in-country stuff advising North Vietnamese units as well as commanding MIKE forces, which were volunteers like the National Guard. These Special Forces formed a project called Delta and that became the model for how we needed to make inserts into enemy territory and gather intelligence. Then they formed two other groups called Project Sigma and Project Omega. Those two were given operational control to SOG in about 1967-1968. They became the genesis of what became the command and control south (CCS).

Throneberry: These units were made of American Special Forces members?

Lindsey: Yes. They were led by Special Forces and small recon teams of 2 or 3 Special Forces men. We also had the "mercenaries" that did not want to serve in the South Vietnamese Army because they were looked down as second class citizens. We would have a team of 3 Special Forces and 4 to 8 of what we called "special commandos."

Throneberry: Tell us about the difficulty you had putting this book together.

Lindsey: This book was written as a memorial to our men because we lost at CCS which is one of the three ground units that had operational control by SOG. We had a northern, central and a southern. We lost about a 100 men and that is both CCS and our air partners. Over a period of time, we had 14 different aviation units, Army and Air Force, that supported us. The way they supported us was we made insertions behind the border in Cambodia by helicopter primarily. Occasionally, we would walk in through the border which was the easiest way because we had 300 miles of border. They would be inserted by either landing the choppers or sometimes they would propel in. That is the way we got in and got out.

Throneberry: The Americans were not allowed to have any identification on us or on the aircraft.

Lindsey: This was a very top secret outfit. It was a dark operation. We were sworn to secrecy. Everyone had to sign that they would not write or tell anything for at least 20 years. So when our men went in, it was in a sterile uniform with no rank or insignia on it. They were told that if they got into trouble, the government would deny any knowledge of them being where they were found. Our people were told that if they got captured to say that they wandered across the border. They kept us top secret for a long time, it was more than 20 years before they finally declassified us. That is why it was so difficult to write this book, the Department of Army destroyed our after-action reports even before they declassified us.

Throneberry: Was it just Army troops that were part of these special teams on the ground?

Lindsey: Army Special Forces troops who were the US component and the others were the mercenaries who were part of the teams and very well trained and heroic individuals who would undertake the most dangerous missions in Vietnam because when they went across the border, they had no artillery, and in Cambodia, we had not tactical air support. All we had was the helicopter gun shift support and we also had an Air Force Unit of helicopters we called the Green Hornets SOS (Special Operations Squadron). They took us in in what we called slicks, which is just a transportation hooah. They had the gunships that could put a wall of fire around us and help us escape.

Throneberry: You mentioned that the lack of support from the Johnson Administration caused some difficulties in what the MACV and SOG were conducting.

Lindsey: That was absolutely true. Special Forces were looked down on at that time by our conventional Army brass, but they didn't have any experience in unconventional warfare. The Geneva Convention that set up the North and South Vietnam situation was one in which Cambodia and Laos were supposed to be neutral and, of course, North Vietnam did not honor that at all. We had an ambassador, I think his name was Sullivan, in Laos and he was given the State Department Authority over what we could do in those two countries. He made very strict conditions on where we could fly, how many people could be there, how many teams on the ground. It was like trying to fight a war with one hand behind your back.

Throneberry: Are there any specific missions you can recall about what some of these men did?

Lindsey: In CCS, we had a fellow there named Mad Dog Shriver because he was so famous by the Vietnamese for getting into their areas and gather intelligence. He was in a mission in an area called The Fishhook, which is just north of Saigon. It's a sand pit. That was where the North Vietnamese headquarters for all of their troops in Cambodia were. So he went in on an operation that was not very well run and he lost his life along with all of his team. My unit had 56 people killed over a 6 year period. My air partner units made up the rest of the total of 100.

Throneberry: Our command and control aircraft was shot down by a SAM missile on October 9, 1969 and we lost people that day. We would take off from a place called Bu Dop and cross the border into Cambodia at a very low level with a team on board. The command and control aircraft would be above us and they would vector the aircraft into an area where they wanted to drop the troops off. We would drop them and get out of there as fast as we could. We were protected by our gunships called The Thunder Chickens. Then we would go back to Bu Dop and wait. They would always run into contact at night and then we would have to go out and get them either by a landing zone or pulling them up by ladders or McGuire rigs, all types of equipment that we needed to get them out safely.

Lindsey: Another story that I can recall led to a medal of honor for one of the pilots. It was the Air Force 20th SOS. We inserted a team and the team ran into a lot of trouble. It was an all day battle trying to get them out. We had lost several helicopters. It was down to one transport slick and one gunship. So we said we were going to do one last try to pull these people out, so Jim Fleming went along a river bank behind the place the battle was taking place and he just landed with his front skins on the river bank and sat there waiting for the team to climb into the chopper. The front plastic bubble of his aircraft was just about shot off and he just sat there calmly as he could. His gunners were supporting the team as they were trying to escape their being surrounded. Anyway, he pulled them out.

Throneberry: These missions were frightening?

Lindsey: They were extremely hazardous. Our guys were volunteered to go to airborne training, then the Special Forces, then to Vietnam and then into SOG. A lot of people chose not to do that, but we had folks in there that had a lot of experience initially but later on in late 1969 and 1970 we were getting people right out of the Special Forces that joined us. These young men just stepped up with some mentoring from the more experienced guys. The best part of what we did, the intelligence of telling our American units along that border when they were going to be hit and who was going to hit them and from what direction. We saved hundreds of lives of American troops that were back behind the border.

Throneberry: I would like you to explain what happened as we were winding down our operations in Vietnam. All the ground troops came home, but there were an awful lot of pilots and Special Forces that stayed there almost to the very end.

Lindsey: That's very true. You will recall when President Nixon came into office with his secret plan that was announced to the world we were going to have an exercise into Cambodia after we had proven beyond a shadow of a doubt that the NVA were in there in division size strength and they were finally given the green light in May and June to go in for 60 days. All of our conventional forces attacked the NVA knew we were coming. Of the units from the teams in our outfit was following a huge trail that was about 40 feet wide that looked like a herd of elephants went through. It was an escaping NVA unit. We stopped them and called B-52 strikes on the people ahead of them.

CHAPTER 7

WHAT IT IS LIKE TO GO TO WAR

Dale Throneberry interviewed Karl Marlantes, who at age 23 in 1968, was dropped into the highland jungle of Vietnam. An inexperienced lieutenant in command of a platoon of 40 Marines who would live or die by his decisions. Marlantes was a bright young man who was well trained for the task at hand but, as he was to discover, far from mentally prepared for what he was about to experience. In *What it is Like to go to War*, Karl Marlantes takes a deeply personal and candid look at the experience and ordeal of combat, critically examining how we might better prepare our young soldiers for war. Marlantes discusses the daily contradictions that warriors face in the grind of war, where each battle requires them to take life or spare life, and where they enter a state he likens to the fervor of religious ecstasy. He makes it clear just how poorly prepared our 19 year old warriors – mainly men but increasingly women – are for the psychological and spiritual aspects of the journey.

September 1, 2012

Throneberry: Karl Marlantes in his 13 month tour, saw intense combat, killed the enemy and watched his friends die. He survived, but like many of his brothers in arms, he spent the last 40 years dealing with his experiences. What made you want to volunteer to go to Vietnam?

Marlantes: The guys that I went into training with, the platoon leaders class of the Marine Corps where you go the first summer of your college year. I had written to the Marine Corps because I got the scholarship, but I thought they would never let me go because by 1967 when I graduated, they were short of second lieutenants. But they did. That first term of 1967, I just felt guilty because the guys that I had been training with were going to Vietnam. I decided to return to the Marines and go to Vietnam.

Throneberry: It didn't seem like there was a really long life expectancy for second lieutenants.

Marlantes: Marine Second Lieutenants are expected to be out in front and Marines have a traditionally different role than other units. They are designed to go fast mainly because the Navy cannot be on shore and it is far easier to replace a Marine than a carrier and so the Marines will take casualties for speed and it's always been that way.

Throneberry: Let's talk about your experiences in Vietnam as a young second lieutenant. You were thrown into combat almost immediately?

Marlantes: It was hardly called combat. I came under fire the day I was choppered in to join my unit. I was just sitting on the floor of the chopper looking out the window at the scenery which was jungle covered mountains and all of the sudden, holes started appearing in the side of the chopper. You couldn't hear anything. Then the chopper went down and crash landed. The crew chief was shouting at us to get out of the chopper. An executive officer came over to me and asked "Have you got the f*** mail?"

Throneberry: The Marines did a good job of training you to be a platoon leader, but they neglected part of your training, don't you think?

Marlantes: It's almost like the culture neglects the training. I'm careful to point out that the Marines are not there to be your spiritual guides, but I think the military could do a better job by being more honest. You look at the advertising and it says, "Join us and you will learn a nice civilian job skill and maybe get a college education." No, no, you are here to kill for your country. You are raised in a Christian culture that, "thou shall not kill." Suddenly, you're expected to kill and nobody is there to help you with that transition which is an enormous moral issue for a decent kid. What do you do when it is suddenly okay to kill and then you come home when it is not okay to kill? As I say in the book, there are wounds from war, wounds to the body, wounds to psyche, but this is a wound to the soul. Particularly, today, they have guys at Dallas Air Force Base commuting from home, back and forth, they are killing Taliban in Afghanistan. This is something we need to think about as a culture, not just the military.

Throneberry: How long would you be out on these patrols without changing?

Marlantes: We would be out 30 days and literally the uniforms would rot off your body. It was months in the clouds. We were up 5,000 feet and it wasn't like the military was starving us or anything. They couldn't find us and we were operating a long way from headquarters. Often we would run out of food. We had actually experienced 5 days without food and about a week on half rations before we hit that time period. We were carrying mortars, mortar plates, ammunition – 80 or 90 pounds per person. We were using ropes to get up and down hills. A person age 45 could not survive this, that's why everyone was around 19. When I was 23, I was the second oldest in the entire company, that's 200+ Marines.

When I started out, there was this very difficult transition between thou shall not kill. There are two ways traditionally that society has resolved this. The first is a way that we have kind of outgrown and that is that God is on our side. The other way that we deal with this is we do it with "pseudospeciating." In other words, we make an animal out of the other person that we have to kill. That way we kind of trick ourselves into the fact that you are not really killing a person. It is very hard to pull that trigger if you think of the person in front of you as a brother of a sister, the son of a mother, you cannot do it unless you say it's a gook and he is trying to kill my friends. The problem with that solution is that years later you wake up in the middle of the night and realize that it wasn't an animal, it was a person.

Throneberry: Can you tell the story of the young soldier in your book?

Marlantes: We were on an assault on a very steep hill and there were 2 NVA soldiers about 20 meters above us. Two hand grenades came flying out. We hit the deck. I got wounded during the first throw. We threw grenades back and forth and then realized we were going to be out of grenades and this was a stupid way to handle this. So I told the guy I was with that when he threw the grenade, I was going to go around the side. I was down on the ground around 10 to 12 feet from this guy. One of the NVA guys in the hole had been killed by our grenades. The other guy rose up to throw another grenade and I was looking at him from across the barrel of my M16 and we locked eyes. I was wishing I could speak Vietnamese and just tell him if you don't throw the grenade, I won't pull the trigger. He just snarled at me and threw the grenade and I pulled the trigger. I had a guy some 20 years later tell me "You had no choice what side you were on. You were born in a logging town in Oregon. That kid was born in a farm village in North Vietnam. You were just playing out your part in this duality of a world we live in. This world of opposites. You had no control. You were on that side, he was on the other. The question I want to ask you, is did you do it with a noble heart?" I started crying. I was trying to kill him as he was trying to kill my friends. I wasn't angry with him, I wasn't trying to borrow

86

money from him. I was just trying to carry out my job as a Marine.
We were told to take the hill and he was trying to kill me and my
friends.

Throneberry: You mentioned that some of the Marines started
taking souvenirs of body parts.

Marlantes: You have to remember, these are 18 and 19 year olds.
They want a letter for their coats, they want a trophy. They started
to move into that savagery that we are capable of. One day, after we
had been fighting for several days, our guys had died and these two
kids cut the ears off of dead NVA that were right in front of them. I
wasn't angry with them because I understood what they were trying
to do, but I just realized that these people aren't human anymore,
this is like taking antlers. I told them they couldn't do that, these
are ears. So to punish them, I made them bury the bodies. They
had to haul the bodies down away from the hills and dig a hold, all
while under fire. One of them started crying and then the other
started crying, when they realized what they had done.

Throneberry: How do you think the military can better prepare
young sailors and marines?

Marlantes: I don't think we need to have full blown courses, maybe
just a few hours of explaining the things that will happen to you.
You are going to take a human life. In training, they don't talk about
the consequences of that. Just simple education would be a big step.

Throneberry: Part of your story was that you were put in charge of this platoon, but you didn't know anybody. You had to earn their respect quickly. How did you go about it?

Marlantes: The first thing is just to admit that you are not God yourself, you don't know everything, you're a rookie. These guys had been there months and they knew a whole lot that you don't get taught at Quantico. So the first thing is make yourself a little humble.

Throneberry: What do you think we could do to better prepare our troops today?

Marlantes: First of all, being able to get educated on these warning signs about when you are losing consciousness of what your mission is. These guys are responsible for a lot of fire power, they are working in a roll of God.

Throneberry: The Vietnam Veterans of America's mantra is, "never again will one generation of veterans ignore another generation of another." I think you will find that the VVA has gone out of their way to try to help these veterans coming back and just provide them the forum where they can talk to somebody.

Marlantes: Some aspects of war don't change. The number one being you are killing people.

Throneberry: You mention in your book to put a face on the enemy. Always remember that they are the son or daughter of someone, husband or wife of someone or the mom or dad of someone.

Now they are going after the VA Hospitals and cutting budgets there, when these people need it the most.

Marlantes: We have to remember that when we send someone to war, their war isn't over when they come home. It's a long-term deal.

CHAPTER 8
LIFE AND TIMES OF A WAR
CORRESPONDENT – JOE GALLOWAY

"Joseph Lee "Joe" Galloway (born November 13, 1941), is an American newspaper correspondent and columnist. Galloway is a native of Refugio, Texas.

He is the former Military Affairs consultant for the Knight-Ridder chain of newspapers and was a columnist with McClatchy Newspapers. During the Vietnam War, he often worked alongside the troops he covered and was awarded a Bronze Star for carrying wounded men to safety.

During the Vietnam War, Galloway worked as a reporter for UPI, beginning in early 1965. Thirty-five years later, he was decorated with the Bronze Star for helping to rescue wounded American soldiers under fire during the battle at Landing Zone X-Ray in the Ia Drang Valley.

Galloway retired as a weekly columnist for McClatchy Newspapers in January 2010, writing, "I have loved being a reporter; loved it when we got it right; understood it when we got it wrong...In the end, it all comes down to the people, both those you cover and those you work for, with or alongside during 50 years.

Along with Lt. Gen. Harold G. Moore, Galloway co-authored a detailed account of those experiences in the best-selling 1992 book, "We Were Soldiers Once... And Young." A sequel was released in 2008: "We Are Soldiers Still: A Journey Back to the Battlefields of Vietnam."

January 24, 2009

Lillie: Joe, you've covered more than the Vietnam War. You've covered a lot of them. How did you start as a journalist? Did you take training or is this something you just jumped into?

Galloway: Oh, no. I think I must have been born one. I worked on the school newspaper in high school. I helped start a competition weekly in my hometown the summer I got out of high school and went off briefly to college. I was driven out by a mayday in class in the German language taught by a portly lady with badly fitting dentures. I was on my way to join the Army, I was 17, I had to browbeat my mother into agreeing to sign for me. We were two blocks from the recruiting office in Victoria, Texas when we passed the local newspaper. Mom said "Joe, what about your journalism?" I said "Good call, Mom, stop the car." I had been their campus stringer for those few weeks and I walked in and asked if the editor had a job, and he did, and he hired me on the spot for $35 per week and a free subscription to the paper. I was on my way.

Lillie: You volunteered for Vietnam. In fact you sent a letter a week. I was doing the same thing at a station in California. I was hounding the personnel office to get any orders to a battalion going to Vietnam. So, you were a journalist elsewhere but you did hound to get over to Vietnam and finally got your wish and ended up in Vietnam. Give us a little bit of history on your first 48 or 72 hours in the country.

Galloway: I landed about two weeks after the Marines. The 1st Battalion 9th Marines landed in Da Nang in March 1965. I landed in April coming from Tokyo. I sort of made a stop there for six months. I got to Saigon on a flight where my seatmate was a little Buddhist monk in an orange robe. The closer we got to Saigon, the more he was talking about sticking to me like glue. I wondered what the heck was going on. We landed and they told everyone to remain in their seats and a squad of white mice (the Saigon Police) got aboard and yanked that Buddhist monk out of his seat and dragged him down the aisle and down the stairs and he was one of those exiles who was trying to slip back in the country and he failed utterly. They put him on the next plane back out. That was my arrival in Vietnam.

I reported in to the old United Press International Bureau and had a day or two in Saigon to get my press card from MACV. Then I got on the mail run, C123 flight that ran from Saigon.

Lillie: Is the Caribou the 123?

Galloway: No, the 123 is a bit bigger than the Caribou. The Caribou was operated by the Army. The 123 was the workhorse, the pre C130. They carried the mail and carried people around. They ran two or three of these flights a day. It took forever to get there but eventually I made it to Da Nang and by then the Marines had taken over a former Merchant Marine brothel on the banks of Da Nang river and turned it into a press center. I had a rented jeep and I lived in Da Nang for six or seven months. I would be up there for two or three months at a time before I would even get back to Saigon. I went on every operation the Marines would let me.

Lillie: You weren't one of those correspondents that recorded the war by sitting back in an air conditioned building and listening to news releases. You were out in the field with the grunts.

Galloway: When I was younger, I had read the collected works of Ernie Pyle and WWII and I decided then, if there was a war during my generation, I wanted to cover it. And if I covered it, I wanted to cover it like Pyle covered his generation. That's up front with the troops and that is precisely what I did. I didn't like Saigon and I didn't like the politics of the situation. I would get to Saigon once in a while and most of the 500+ accredited correspondents spent their time in Saigon. They went to the daily briefings, we called them the "5 o'clock follies", and they would complain to me that they were lying to us. My answer was always the same, no one lies to you within the sound of the guns. You come out with me and people tell you the truth.

Lillie: Tell us about your first time you went out with the troops.

Galloway: It was on the day I arrived. I got off that plane and a fellow ran up to me and said "I am Raua, I work for UPI, there is big trouble, come with me." I was carrying a Samsonite suitcase and still wearing chinos and loafers. I hadn't even gotten a set of fatigues yet. I said "What about my suitcase?" and he said something rude about it and threw it in the 8th Aerial Transport Squadron hooch at Da Nang and dragged me on a C130 that was spinning up on the ramp. I didn't know where I was going or what was going on. We made a short flight and we landed in a place called Quang Ngai City. We got off and it was like someone had stirred an ant hill.

They were under serious attack and serious pressure in that area. It was an early attempt by the Viet Cong to cut the country in half. I got off and there was confusion all around, planes and choppers coming and going, people running around. This photographer ran off to a Marine H34, an old titanium magnesium based helicopter, and he talked to the crew chief and then he waved at me and the next thing I know, I'm on this bird and we are flying out at a low level across the patties. I still don't know where I am and I still don't know where I'm going. This helicopter finally comes upon a hill that rises out of the rice patties and it circled around this hill. I'm trying to look out the door and I can see there are a lot of people on top of this hill. We land there and they shut down, and there is dead silence. I got out of the bird and then I was told why they were giving us this ride. They needed our help. A battalion of South Vietnamese had been overrun and killed to the last man and we were there to help them find and bring back the bodies of the two American advisors. They had only time to sort of scratch out a little body depression in the ground and every man was laying where he had made his last stand, hands out like he was holding a rifle but the rifle was gone. We went hole to hole until we found the two Americans and carried them back to the helicopter. It was a very sobering welcome to Vietnam.

Lillie: You spent so much time in war that when the troops were going into Iraq, Knight-Ridder Newspaper asked you to write a memo to the correspondents that would be traveling along with them, to give them advice. In reading your memo, it was amazing, down to the simple things, a big neckerchief. Tell us why they would want a big neckerchief.

Galloway: You need to bathe in it for one thing. It's your towel, it's your neck rag, but mainly in the desert, you wear it across your face like a bank robber to keep the sand out of your mouth.

Lillie: A good set of ear plugs?

Galloway: You ride helicopters a lot in the combat operation and they're bad on your ears. I'm probably half deaf anyway, if not three quarters deaf.

Lillie: You said, if things start happening, if anyone tells you to move out, or run, or dig a hole, do so with vigor.

Galloway: Yes indeed. If stuff starts coming in and things start blowing up, and you don't know what to do, find someone with stripes on his arm and do what he does.

Lillie: One of the things you said in combat, they may find they need a helping hand. You've done this a lot, carry water, or ammo or the dead if needed.

Galloway: That's correct and I've done all of those things. You have to make yourself of some use besides standing around like a bump on a log.

Lillie: When you first got to Vietnam, you were also carrying a weapon. How did that happen?

Galloway: Not when I first got there, but not long after, there were battalion commanders who would tell you straight up, "Look here, I don't have the spare bodies to give you your personal bodyguard. You have to take care of yourself. If you are not carrying a weapon, you can't march with my outfit." Second of all, in spite of the fact that you carried a press card and it had real fine print on the back of it that said that you were to be treated with all the privileges afforded a Major in the US Army if you were captured by enemies of the United States. I didn't recall if they were very kind to anyone of any rank if you fell into the hands of the enemies. Besides, they were shooting at me. I felt obliged, on occasion, to shoot back.

Lillie: After getting your first weapon, you went to Plei Me Camp, a Special Forces camp, and met up with Major Beckwith and got an even more powerful weapon.

Galloway: It was the third week of October 1965 and Plei Me Camp was under siege by a regiment of the North Vietnamese and they were holding the camp hostage as dangling bait to draw the South Vietnamese armored column up the road to rescue them and they had another regiment standing by to ambush them. I wanted to get in there and the air space was closed. A couple of Huey helicopters had been shot down, a sky raider and a bomber, the place had those 51 caliber Chinese anti-aircraft machine guns on tripods and they were looking down our throats.

I was stomping up and down the flight line at Camp Holloway saying rude words and things and I ran across an old Texas helicopter pilot, a Huey pilot with the 119th helicopter company. He said, "What's the matter Joe?" I said, "Well, I'm trying to get into Plei Me Camp and there is no way to go." He said, "Let me get the clipboard." He took a look and said, "The reason you can't get in there, is the air space is closed." I said, "I know that, dummy, but I still want in there." He said, "I wouldn't mind taking a look, so I will give you a ride." Rayburns flew me in there. He hit the ground. I took a picture. We were corkscrewing to avoid those machine guns and dropping in as fast as he could and I shot a picture out the open doorway. You can see the triangular shaped camp filling that doorway in the picture. You can see the smoke from mortar bombs going off and that is where we were headed. He brought that thing in and I bailed out. We threw some wounded aboard and off he went. This Master Sergeant Special Forces came up to me and said, "Sir, I don't know who the heck you are, but Major Beckwith wants to speak to you right away." I said, "Which one is he?" He said, "It's that big guy over there jumping up and down on his hat." He said a lot of rude words we can't say on this network but he said "Who are you?" I said, "I'm a reporter." He said, "You know I need everything in the whole f*** world. I need medevac, I need food, I could use reinforcements, I need ammo. I need everything. I could use a bottle of Jim Bean and a box of cigars. And what has the Army and its wisdom sent me but a f*** reporter? I got to tell you, son, I have no vacancy for a reporter, but I'm in desperate need of a corner machine gunner, and you're it!" My mouth was hanging open by then. He hauled me over to a position and there was air cool 34 caliber machine gun sitting there and he showed me how to load it, how to clear a jam, and he gave me my instructions which was that I should shoot all the little brown men outside the wire but not the ones inside the wire, they belong to him. He said, "While you are at, keep one eye always on that machine gun positioned all the way down in the other corner of the camp. Because it's manned by South Vietnamese CIDG, they're infiltrated, I don't trust them as far as I can throw them. If you see them turn that machine gun around, take them out."

I spent three days and three nights with that machine gun, it was what you call "sporting times." Finally, the armored column made it through the ambush, thanks to the 1st Cav hopscotching artillery batteries which were slung beneath Chinook helicopters. This was something new in this war and the North Vietnamese didn't know about it and when they snapped their ambush, they got hammered by precise artillery fire and they got hammered by a whole world of air.

Lillie: These were tactics that they used against the French quite successfully. Setting up a bait like Plei Me Camp, not taking it on purpose, and setting up ambushes to wipe out the column.

Galloway: The one thing that was different here was that the First Calvary Division had arrived. They had 435 helicopters and they could guarantee that South Vietnamese armor commander was refusing to leave Pla Que until the Calvary guaranteed he would be under an umbrella of artillery protection every mile of the way. They pulled in and then a battalion of the First Calvary did air soft landing and were marching off to clear the hills around the camp.

Lillie: Who was in command of that unit?

Galloway: I don't remember which battalion it was. I went to Major Beckwith and said my goodbyes. He said, "Son, you're not carrying a piece." I said, "Well, you know, technically speaking, I'm a civilian non-combatant under the Geneva Conventions in spite of the use you have made of me these last three days and nights. He said, "There's no such thing in these mountains. Master Sergeant, get the man a rifle and a bag of magazines." I marched out of there with an M16 on my shoulder and a sack of magazines fully loaded. Three weeks later, I would thank my lucky stars and thank Major Charlie Beckwith who was a friend of mine to his last days, for that rifle.

Lillie: When you got out into the hills, what did you find?

Galloway: Incredible. The hills were stripped of vegetation. There were a few trees still standing, most of the branches gone, all of the leaves gone, but the soil looked like it had been plowed by a giant plow or something. Nothing was left unturned, untouched, and we found North Vietnamese machine gunners' bodies with the leg chained to the tripod of their gun. Later I had occasion to interview General Ohn, who was the technical commander at X-ray and in this fight too. We interviewed him three times. I asked him about that. He tried to avoid the question, but I pushed as I tend to do, and he said, "Look, it was the 32nd regime and they were fairly green and we knew they were going to be subject to heavy, heavy air attack, and we were afraid they would run. So we just fixed it so they couldn't." Those guys stayed with their guns and died with their guns.

Lillie: That is something you won't see in the American military. We covered the Battle of LZ X-ray before, but I've had a lot of requests. In the movie, Sergeant Major Plumbley came up to you and you were hugging the ground under fire, what did he do?

Galloway: Just as it was in the movie, I'm laying in there feathering out at the edges, staying real low, there is a world of fire coming right through the command post area and I can't get low enough. About then, I feel this lump in my ribs and I carefully turn my head without lifting it to see what it is, and what it is, is a size 12 combat boot on the foot of Sergeant Major Plumbley. Bent over at the waist and over this den of battle, he shouted down at me and said, "Can't take no pictures laying there on the ground sonny."

Lillie: And that was portrayed in the movie. I wondered myself, did it really happen?

Galloway: Absolutely. I laid there and thought, well, he is right. Later on I would learn that Sergeants and Majors are always right. Like a fool, I got up and I thought maybe we are all going to die here today and if I'm going to get mine, I would rather take it standing along the side of a man like Major Plumbley.

Lillie: Joe, you've covered more wars and more battles. Who was it that said you have more time in combat than any infantrymen?

Galloway: That was General Barry McCaffery.

Lillie. He's right, correct?

Galloway: I don't know, there were a lot of guys, with a lot of time in combat now with 3 or 4 tours in Iraq and Afghanistan. So, I don't know if that stands or not. I'm happy to let that record go to somebody else.

Lillie: You did some more tours of Vietnam after that first tour with LZ X-ray. Were there other battles in that first tour that equaled it?

Galloway: None that ever equaled it, not in that tour or three other tours that I pulled in Vietnam, not in a half dozen other wars I've covered. That was a high watermark and it was the bloodiest battles of the Vietnam War. Right then, right there. 305 American boys killed in that campaign. Hundreds and hundreds wounded. Just a ferocious collision between the two finest light infantry outfits operating in the world. The North Vietnamese Army and the First Calvary Division.

Lillie: I've heard many grunts say that the North Vietnamese Army, their troops were very good at what they did. Well-trained, well-armed, well-equipped and dedicated.

Galloway: Absolutely. They weren't afraid to die. They had to walk to work through a firestorm just to get to us. They didn't flinch. They were superb infantry fighters and anyone who didn't respect that enemy in Vietnam was an absolute fool or dead.

Lillie: Politics aside, when you left Vietnam for the last time, what was your impression of the American soldier?

Galloway: My impression of the American soldier in Vietnam in 1965, '71, '73, of the American Soldier in the Gulf War, in Haiti, and two tours in Iraq, I have the highest respect for American Soldiers. There is a difference between soldiers who fought in Vietnam and those who fight today in Iraq and Afghanistan, the volunteer Army. These kids are more sophisticated. They are better educated, better trained and certainly better armed. Soldiering comes down to matter of the heart. That is unchanging. I think it has never changed from the first day a guy picked up a rock to defend his cave and his wife and his kids, over 10,000 years ago. There is a sense about the soldier of selfless sacrifice. He isn't in it for the glory. There is no glory in combat. There is no glory in war. It's a hard, bloody task that will leave you carrying the burden of memories of things that no one should see, especially when you are 18 or 19 years old. The soldiers are the same. I've counted it a privilege to have been allowed to stand beside them then, to stand beside them today, and they are my brothers. What can I say?

Lillie: I hear this phrase over and over again and it messes with my mind, they say, "I was just doing my job." I can't process that. Is there any way that you can put it down in words that will allow me and others that I know to process that?

Galloway: What they are saying is that the training took over in the heat of battle, in the worse of combat, you're training is what will save your life. You start doing things automatically because it is almost impossible to think. The smoke, the confusion, men dying all around you, people screaming for their mother, it is just that – the training and a modesty. I can't tell you how many times I have interviewed soldiers, fighter pilots, they will sit there for hours and tell you what the guy on their left did, what the guy on their right did, and they don't want to tell you what they did. They are modest heroes - our soldiers, our marines, our airmen, our sailors, our coastguard guys.

Lillie: Our own Dale Throneberry was a helicopter pilot over there and he did something that was just remarkable and I wanted to do a program on slicks, the helicopter pilots. I wanted him to tell a story about how he got his helicopter down through a triple canopy jungle, having to go from hole to hole in the canopies to get a wounded grunt off the ground. He said, "I jiggled around a little bit and went down and got this guy." I almost dove across the table and grabbed him by the throat.

Galloway: Helicopter pilots are not necessarily the most modest of men. I've heard some tales from them that you have to take with a grain of salt, but they are great soldiers. They always came when you called. You call, we haul. They used to have cards with it printed on them. I hated them when they dropped me off in some God awful place where people were trying to kill me, but they would come back to get you when it was all over. I loved them when they gave me a ride out.

Lillie: They were heroes. The guys that went in there like the guy that took you into Plei Me and the guy that took you into LZ X-ray.

Galloway: Bruce Crandall earned a righteous Medal of Honor. I rode in his chopper, into X-ray and three days later, I rode in his chopper out.

Lillie: How many choppers did he go through in that first night?

Galloway: I think he went through three. Bruce and I are still best friends today. You make friends in a situation like that in a battlefield and if you can find them after the war is over, you got a friend for life. I'm so thankful that I was allowed to survive to write the stories, to tell the stories, to try to tell the truth about the American soldier. No finer, more noble creature, in my view, than just your plain, ordinary grunt existing in a hell that is combat and somehow making it through, taking care of his brothers on the right and left, never worrying about himself, willing to stand up and go to certain death trying to save a friend or buddy. A buddy he doesn't even know.

CHAPTER 9
FORWARD AIR CONTROLLER
PILOT LT. COL. JONATHAN MEYER

"Forward air control is the provision of guidance to Close Air Support (CAS) aircraft intended to ensure that their attack hits the intended target and does not injure friendly troops. This task is carried out by a forward air controller (FAC).

The rugged jungle terrain of South East Asia readily hid enemy troop movements. U.S. fighter-bombers were so fast that pilots had great difficulty in distinguishing between enemy troops, friendly troops, and civilians. Forward air controllers directing air strikes thus became essential in usage of air power.

Visual reconnaissance formed the core FAC mission during the Vietnam War, as the FAC flew light aircraft slowly over the rough terrain at low altitude to maintain constant aerial surveillance. By patrolling the same area constantly, the FACs grew very familiar with the terrain, and they learned to detect any changes that could indicate enemy forces hiding below.

Tracks on the ground, misplaced vegetable patches, an absence of water buffalo, smoke from cooking fires in the jungle, too many farmers working the fields—all could indicate enemy troops in the area.

Flying low and slow over enemy forces was very dangerous; however the enemy usually held his fire to avoid discovery.

Each of the O-1 FAC aircraft originally used carried three different radios for coordinating with everyone involved in an air strike: an FM radio for the ground forces, a UHF radio for the fighter aircraft, and a VHF radio for contact with the Air Force Tactical Air Control Party to coordinate approvals and requests for air support.

The FAC radioed for strike aircraft after spotting the enemy. He marked the target with smoke grenades or white-phosphorus rockets to pinpoint targets. After directing the fighter-bombers' attacks, the FAC would fly low over the target to assess the damage."

November 21, 2009

Lillie: Lt. Col. Jonathan Meyer you were born in London England, how did you end up in our military?

Meyer: I came over to America at the age of 16 to go to college here. I took up my citizenship in 1953. ROTC commission.

Lillie: You flew F86's at one point?

Meyer: The L model, the interceptor version.

Lillie: Then you ended up going to a plane that was operated a lot slower and a lot lower – the FAC. How did that come about? Tell us what a FAC is?

Meyer: A FAC is a forward air controller. The L19, to use its old name "Old One" as we called it, was the single engine airplane that was flying forward air controlled during the early years of the war. There were 2 others: the O2 and the OV10 that came along later. When it was my turn to go to Southeast Asia, I went from an F101B interceptor squadron to the O1 to be a forward air controller.

Lillie: That plane was designed after WWII to replace the old canvas covered version.

Meyer: I believe it was made in the early 1950's and the Army flew it for some years before the rest of the services got their share.

Lillie: Was the plane a 1 seater or 2 seater?

Meyer: It could be flown by one but could carry an observer in the back or another pilot. They were in tandem seats (front and back). It was a high wing, single engine, 6 pitch propeller at the time. We had good visibility out of the airplane, but it was slow and low and that's how we did our job.

Lillie: I'm assuming you got shot at a bit while you were down there?

Meyer: A few times. Only got hit once though. Probably a lot less than average.

Lillie: Did you volunteer for this or were you assigned to it?

Meyer: No. I was assigned. As far as I was concerned, it was sort of an interruption in my supersonic jet flying, but I hadn't been over in Vietnam for more than 2 or 3 weeks when I became a very strong believer in what we were trying to do over there and it stayed that way ever since.

Lillie: What was your reaction when you learned that's what you were going to do and what was your training like?

Meyer: Reaction was sort of aghast, but orders are orders. I went down and checked out this airplane and how it feels in the Florida Panhandle.

Lillie: Over and above training on the plane, did they train you in observation?

Meyer: As much as we could be. It was visual recognizance. We were depended upon day time, good weather conditions, to be able to see anything. We didn't have much in the way of sensors except binoculars from time to time. We were just basically trying to circle around our province or sector to see what, if anything, we could see on the ground. This was not always easy in the central highlands because there was a lot of mountainous terrain and foliage.

Lillie: Did it take a while to get your eyes, at first, it's all jungle, and after a little bit of experience you would be able to pick things up a little better?

Meyer: Of course, experience always helps.

Lillie: Did you get calls from the guys on the ground?

Meyer: Sure, from time to time. Usually, in our province, we worked to a fair degree, with Special Forces A team camps. I would contact the camp any time I was in the vicinity. Occasionally, I would get a call from a patrol on the ground wanting to know something or tell me something. That's how we maintained contact, over flex mike radio, FM frequency.

Throneberry: I was a helicopter pilot in Vietnam and we used you guys many times. I was down in III Corps between the Parrots Beak and the Fishhook, and many of our missions were one ship missions and you guys would go out and prep our landing zones to make sure that the bad guy kept their head down for a little bit. I want to thank you for all of the helicopter pilots out there for the work that you did over there in protecting us.

Meyer: I put in a few, what they call LZ or landing zone preps where we would push in a flight or two of fighters to bomb around the general area that was planned for landing to make sure there were no ambushes waiting.

Lillie: You guys were basically unarmed, but how did you mark a target and what did you carry for self-protection?

Meyer: The target locking was by Willie Pete or white phosphorous rocket. On my time, we had two on each wing so we had four marking shots and those would set up a cloud of white smoke. We also had smoke grenades, where if you couldn't see the flat range, you could fly over it and perhaps pick it up and drop a grenade out your side window. For self-protection, we really didn't have much except sitting on our parachutes or sitting on life vests and M16 for survival, and usually a shiny 6 shooter revolver.

Lillie: On firing your Willie Pete rockets, how did you aim those rockets?

Meyer: It was a matter of lining up the area that you want to hit with about the second stud on the center of the windshield and hosing one off.

Lillie: So in other words, you had to point the airplane where you wanted the rocket to go?

Meyer: Right.

Lillie: I don't know how you guys hit anything.

Meyer: It was often a gamble. You simply adjust anybody's bombing run from the position of your smoke. If you hit right on, you would say hit my smoke. If you needed to move 50 meters one way or another, that's how you would do it.

Lillie: When you said you had to move 50 meters, is that because you had visual contact with the bad guys on the ground?

Meyer: If one had the visual contact, that's what we would do. If it was a matter of hitting the certain areas where we thought the enemy was or that we had been directed to hit an intelligence generated target, it really made no difference. We would use the same basic technique.

Lillie: I had a friend who was a FAC pilot. He told me that he would be up there and his orders would be to take off from the Da Nang Airport, take a heading of 270, 1 ½ miles, mark the target and step aside. How do you actually know you are hitting anywhere near something? A couple of times, he found the enemy in the open and would radio in and they would say, "Acknowledge, proceed on mission." Did you see anything of that nature?

Meyer: I personally did not. If one is given a target through the intel process, they normally give it in coordinates and you would

113

find that area on your map, which is an artillery chart of 1 to 50,000 scale and aim your fire according to that. You might not even know what you are hitting. Sometimes if you hit an enemy storage place, you might set off what they called a secondary explosion as you hit something and it blew up. Usually, the fighters would do the actual striking.

Lillie: How often would you have that type of success?

Meyer: It was rare.

Lillie: You flew nighttime missions?

Meyer: In the DMZ when I was up there for 3 ½ weeks with Operation Tallyho, we flew around the clock.

Lillie: What was Tallyho?

Meyer: It was sort of a project and also the area in Route Package I or the demilitarized zone that separated north and south Vietnam. Because of the infiltration across the border from the north to the south, as well as down the Ho Chi Minh Trail through Laos, they set up this Tallyho operation where we had Bird Dogs doing day and night surveillance and conducting air strikes if they found anything that looked suspicious or that we were directed to look for.

Lillie: The Bird Dog is what you called your plane, the L19 or L1. Did everyone refer to their observation planes as Bird Dogs?

Meyer: Only the ones that flew the Bird Dogs or when the Bird Dog was flying. If it was a different airplane, the O2 or the OV10, they had different call signs and different times and places.

Lillie: A Bird Dog is really like a piper cub. If you went out to your local civilian airport, you could probably see a lot of them that look just like the Bird Dog.

Meyer: This is true except that mostly the airplanes these days have tricycle landing gear. We had a tail wheel. It's that old in terms of design.

Lillie: Trying to get people to understand how primitive these things are, when you were talking about reading your map, you are trying to fly your airplane and the map is like the old map you're your dad used to use for the trips across the country and you would open that up and find that the coordinates or wherever the area is that you were going to, continuing to fly and looking at the map and looking out the window. There wasn't anything like GPS in those days.

Meyer: We were basically out of range or line of sight of any kind of attack and station so we had the radials and circles marked on our maps that we could direct fighters according to that as a reference. They were no good to us in the central highlands when I was flying.

Lillie: On the internet I came across a photograph that was a 101st Airborne camp out in the field where they did have tents. Two guys took cover in their bunker because of incoming, it was nighttime, it was actually their tent. When they woke in the morning, there was a Bird Dog right next to them and it was so tight that the wing tip was over their tent. This guy had received damage and so he landed right there on the rough ground because there was no airstrip there. The next morning, they looked the plane over and decided they thought they could make it and so he took off and I think he left his observer behind to get out another way.

When you were getting contact on the ground, did you ever get contact from troops that were under fire that really need help?

Meyer: Yes. That was one of the missions I happened to fly. It turned out that I was the guy in the air at the time and there was a patrol that had gone out of our Special Forces B team to a village about 20 odd clicks to the north (that's kilometers) and they, in effect, wound up fighting a reinforced company and called for help and I was able to put in several strikes all around them. It turned out from later debriefs that we actually got 28 KIAs on the enemies' side. That was one occasion that troops were under fire and I came to their aide.

Lillie: For the audience, a B team versus a reinforced company, what would the odds be?

Meyer: This B team patrol was about 30 people strong led by a couple of Special Forces NCOs. Sergeant Rockford was the man and the rest of his troops were largely Vietnamese strikers who would be trained by the Special Forces to help defend their areas. Reinforced company would be something over 100 people and that is what they ran up against.

Lillie: A friend of mine was a radio relay operator that would set up on a hilltop and relay the transmissions from out in the field back to the artillery. He said one of the things that was tough was trying to get the guys in the field to calm down so they could get coordinates. If you could imagine, they were under intense attack or an intense

117

fire fight. What was the sound to this B team from these Special Forces guys? What this calm, excited...?

Meyer: They sounded somewhat excited as one naturally would be, but they certainly were not panic stricken or anything like that. They are professionals and doing their job. I was only too happy to oblige and give whatever help I could.

Lillie: I want to keep stressing how good the troops were over there and today.

Meyer: And today especially. They are my heroes.

Lillie: Dale, these FAC pilots were awfully brave people.

Throneberry: When you think about how low and slow they were going, it's amazing what they were able to do.

Lillie: Jonathan, you guys had a Medal of Honor recipient as a FAC pilot. Tell us about this man who won the Medal of Honor.

Meyer: Nobody wins it. There were 2 FACs who were awarded the Medal of Honor. Both of them posthumously. One was a classmate of mine in FAC school – Hilliard A. "Willie" Willbanks. That was during my time. The other was Stephen Bennett, the OV10, a few years later. Willie was the one who affected me the most and as far as I'm concerned, the count was that he saved approximately about 134 Vietnamese rangers and their US Army ranger advisors from an ambush by the north Vietnamese, something close to a regiment of troops who were lying in wait for them.

Lillie: What did he do, can you expand on that a bit?

Meyer: He was familiar with that particular area when no one had been able to find this enemy unit. He knew where to look, spotted them, couldn't get any air support in time, and to protect the ARVIN troops (that's Army of Republic of Vietnam Rangers and their advisors), and he started making passes at the enemy force. First, firing his Willie Pete rockets. When he ran out of those, he started shooting his M16 at them out the window and they, of course, were firing back and eventually hit him and brought him down and he died.

Lillie: He was alive when they got to him finally, right?

Meyer: Just barely. But he died on the way back in a helicopter to medical attention.

Lillie: This was a classmate of yours?

Meyer: Yes.

Lillie: What about the other Medal of Honor recipient? Do you know the story on him?

Meyer: Only broadly. I'm not the authority. He had, I believe, a Marine in the backseat and when they took a hit, he wanted to eject both of them but the guy in the back had his parachute shredded so Steve Bennett decided to make a water landing in the OV10 knowing full well that it wasn't really a survivable process, but he saved his backseater at the cost of his own life.

Lillie: The unselfishness.

Lille: Switching to a lighter topic. So you saw pink elephants, tell us about those.

Meyer: They were pink and people didn't believe me when I got down and told them about it. A few days later, I had an Army observer in my backseat. We flew to the same area and he said "By golly, they sure are pink." And that's how my song ends. His name was Gary Winetier.

Lillie: Give us an explanation of why those elephants were pink.

Meyer: The story was, and by the way other FACs reported that they too had seen pink elephants, was that they would roll in the mud and the earth was sort of reddish around the highlands and elsewhere and when it dried, it would dry sort of red on grey, which muted out to pink.

Lillie: Who was the bravest person you saw over there?

Meyer: It had to be Hilliard Willbanks, though I didn't see him after we left the United States. I knew where he was and heard about his last mission and death about 2 days before I was rotating for home, which was a very unpleasant surprise and since then I've got to know his family. One other thought is the helicopter pilots who came to Hilliard's rescue have never been truly recognized even in the Air Force magazine story. John Groe is perhaps the chief among them and Jerry Borquin, last known out in California. John Groe took about 52 or so hits in his helicopter trying to rescue Hilliard.

Lillie: He wasn't successful in that was he?

Meyer: No. They managed to medevac him out a little later but it just shows you the bravery of the helicopter pilots like the Raven FACs, the F105 pilots over the north, the F4 pilots, just about everyone that flew. Depending on what you were flying and where, and what time of which year, you're fortunes could be totally different.

Throneberry: It didn't make any difference who you were or what branch of the service you were in, if it was an American that went down, we would go get him. We didn't care.

Meyer: If the troops are in trouble, we let it all hang out to go and help them.

Throneberry: Discretion was not the better part of valor sometimes.

Meyer: If the VC could have shot straight while I was there, I probably wouldn't have made it home either.

Lillie: When you get picked up in an aircraft and say, "Where are we?"

Throneberry: Yeah, we did that a few times. We landed in the wrong LZ more than once, unfortunately, and you think there is nobody here. And they said we are 50 clicks to the north, south, east or west. And we would say that it looks just like the field you described to us because we would do all of our stuff low level. It happened. And you are adaptable. That is one of the things about American Forces, that we are resilient, and we think, and help each other.

Lillie: What is your proudest feeling of what you did, Jonathan?

Meyer: I was convinced when I got home that I had the best job in the war because I not only got to see a bit of the country, and visit some of the camps and villages, and work with the military on the ground, that was the most rewarding. Being able to help people that were really in trouble and just simply take the risks. I was not doing anything deliberately stupid, at least not most of the time, and I was just glad to be able to help. That was what I thought was the most important thing.

Lillie: When someone got into trouble on the ground, would it be the nearest FAC that would head there and what would happen with the jet fighters?

Meyer: It was a general rule that's what would happen, and whichever FAC either got the word or was nearest, would sort of immediately go there, take over and be back on the scene. Meanwhile, he would be radioing or fighters would already be ordered to respond, and this is what we would call an immediate air strike with troops in contact, PICs. Those were the ones where people just dropped everything and went to do what was necessary. The FAC put the fighters in, give them the information, controlled the air battle as it was, and let the fighters do the work. They were usually fighters. They were sometimes light bombers. They would try to take care of business and help whoever was on the ground.

Lillie: Give us a wrap up of the things you saw over there.

Meyer: Most of my tour was spent doing visual reconnaissance. Whenever necessary or whenever scheduled, was putting in air strikes or conducting some operation that would support ground troops. But there were lots of other things we did.

Lillie: I want to tell the story of my friend Dick Root. He was the line company officer in the Army and ended up becoming a FAC. He was the backseater to you guys. One time, flying low and slow, they got shot down and his pilot put it down in a clearing and it was kind of a semi-controlled landing in which the plane crumpled up and both of them were jammed inside the cockpit and the bad guys started coming out of the woods at them and they were defending themselves with that little folding M16 that you guys carried. Then the helicopter gunships showed up and then the other aircraft, keeping the bad guys away. They were eventually cut out of the airplane and rescued by a helicopter crew. As he told the story, he kept getting angrier and angrier, and he said "Dirty %#&* shot us down, broke both of my legs, then they tried to kill us."

Meyer: The irony is that if you don't get hurt, killed or badly scared, war can be a most enjoyable, sometimes addictive operation. I sometimes would fly low after an air strike, sort of trolling for gunfire. The fighters wondered why I did it. I was pretty sure there was nothing down there, but just to show them that if we could drum up a little more business, they would have something else to shoot at.

Lillie: I tell people I fell in love with the American people in Vietnam because it seemed the more miserable things got, the funnier people got.

Listen to **Veterans Radio** to hear about the stories and issues facing veterans today, and tales from battles past. Tune in online at VeteransRadio.net and Like them on Facebook at www.Facebook.com/VeteransRadio.

www.VeteransRadio.net

You can call us at

(844) 838-1600

LEGAL HELP FOR VETERANS, PLLC

A PROUD SPONSOR OF VETERANS RADIO

www.LegalHelpForVeterans.com

Facebook.com/legalhelpforveterans

Call today for a free claim review

(800) 693-4800

Fighting exclusively for veterans' rights since 1998. Unlike other law firms, we concentrate only on veterans' disability claims. We fight to make sure you get the benefits you deserve from the Department of Veterans Affairs.

We are proud to be the newest partner of Veterans Radio.

"It is our duty

to protect those

who protected us."

~ Brigadier General

Carol Ann Fausone (Ret.)